Turkish delights

John Gregory-Smith is a chef and food writer who specialises in Turkish cuisine. He is passionate about Turkey having explored the country extensively over the last 10 years and regularly hosts Turkish pop-ups and secret supper clubs in London.

This is John's third book and follows the success of *Mighty Spice Cookbook* and *Mighty Spice Express*. He is the founder of online magazine *Eat Travel Live*, a weekly columnist for *Grazia* and has presented programmes on TV in both the UK and USA.

Turkish delights

Stunning regional recipes
from the Bosphorus to the Black Sea

John Gregory-Smith
Food photography by Martin Poole

Kyle Books

Murat bey, I love you very much

First published in Great Britain in 2015 by Kyle Books, an imprint of Kyle Cathie Ltd 192–198 Vauxhall Bridge Road London SW1V 1DX general.enquiries@kylebooks.com www.kylebooks.co.uk

10 9 8 7 6 5 4 3 2

ISBN 978 0 85783 298 6

John Gregory-Smith is hereby identified as the author of this work in accordance with Section 77 of the Copyright, Designs and Patents Act 1988.
All rights reserved.

Project Editor: Tara O'Sullivan
Copy Editor: Abi Waters
Designer: Ruth Tyson
Food Photographer: Martin Poole
Food Stylist: Rosie Reynolds
Prop Stylist: Wei Tang
Production: Nic Jones and Gemma John

A Cataloguing in Publication record for this title is available from the British Library.
Colour reproduction by ALTA London
Printed and bound in China by C&C Offset Printing Co., Ltd.

contents

Black Sea

MARMARA

Istanbul

Sea of
Marmara

BLACK
SEA

Bursa

Ankara

CENTRAL
ANATOLIA

İzmir

Alaçati

Ephesus

AEGEAN

Konya

Aegean
Sea

MEDITERRANEAN

Mediterranean Sea

Samsun

Trabzon

EAST ANATOLIA

Lake Van

SOUTHEAST ANATOLIA

Gaziantep

Adana

Turkey

With so many wonderful regions and food so deeply steeped in culture and history, it is easy to be inspired by the cuisine of this magnificent country.

I first visited Turkey ten years ago with my father, who was brought up there. When he was a boy, he lived in Ankara, the capital of Turkey, in Central Anatolia, and he has beautiful black and white photos of family holidays to Ephesus, an Ancient Greek city on the Ionian coast, in the 1950s. He remembers the food of his home country only too well, and I've certainly inherited his love for this exquisite cuisine. On that first visit, I took my dad to Çiya, a kebab restaurant on a busy backstreet on the Asia side of Istanbul, surrounded by vibrant shops selling piles of fresh herbs, vegetables, nuts, dried fruits, coffee and olive oil.

The menu at Çiya was very eastern Turkish, with stews, *meze*, kebabs and incredible homemade breads. They had a small display of tempting food laid out canteen-style as we walked in and a great wood-fired oven crackling away at the back.

We sat outside the restaurant, chatting in the sunshine and waiting for our food. I knew I must be in for a treat, but I was unprepared for just how good it was. I had ordered their speciality, the Çiya kebab. It was a minced beef kebab wrapped in thin pastry with mint, a stringy, mozzarella-like cheese (*lor peyniri*) and walnuts. The kebab was baked until golden and served with yogurt.

Tasting the first bite of that kebab was a real revelation for me – it was so delicious.

We also ate *meze* salads, stuffed dried aubergines, *içli köfte* (a fried meatball *köfte*), okra cooked in tomato and garlic, lentil soup and a wonderful chicken *pilav* that was baked in a dough case and turned out at the table. At first glance, it looked like a traditional British suet pudding, but as I broke into the crispy golden pastry the aromas of black pepper, allspice and cinnamon wafted up. A perfect *pilav* was inside, beautifully spiced, with shredded chicken and almonds. What a feast. I had fallen for Turkish food – and good God, I had fallen hard.

I was hooked, and so began years of trips to Turkey to discover more about the cuisine, along with hours dining in the Turkish restaurants of East London – thank you Mangal and Tas Tirin. My cupboards became stocked with Turkish ingredients as I explored more and more traditional recipes. My father was thrilled with my new-found love for the flavours of his childhood, and I loved hearing his memories. It helps that my partner, Murat, is also Turkish, and together we have had many great adventures discovering more of his beautiful home country.

the melting pot

It is the history of this part of the world that makes Turkish cuisine so interesting.

Turkey is a vast country of dramatically varying yet stunningly beautiful landscapes. Enormous, snow-capped mountains dominate the east, huge, lake-covered plains make up the centre, and tall pine forests roll down into the Black Sea in the north. The Mediterranean and the Aegean Sea hug the southern and western coasts. Here, the temperature is blissful, the rugged coves give way to white sandy beaches and the hills are littered with oregano-scented stone villages. Further up the coast lies Istanbul, one of the great cities of the world and the bridge between Europe and the East.

Turkish people are very warm and welcoming. Family is extremely important to them – and so is food. Hugely varied, it covers everything from freshly cooked light coastal cuisine to fiery eastern kebabs and opulent Ottoman dishes.

It is the history of this part of the world that makes Turkish cuisine so interesting. Turkey is a relatively new country, born on 29th October 1923, when Atatürk founded The Republic of Turkey, ending the 600-year-old Ottoman Empire. Before this, the Lycians, Persians, Ancient Greeks, Romans and Byzantines all passed through, conquering and falling. Turkey was the link between East and West and the bridge of the Silk Road, which saw spices and other precious cargoes transported across Europe. Each culture brought their religions, customs and food, which were absorbed like a sponge into this melting pot of a country.

The Ottoman Empire had been one of the largest in the world – the sultans reigned over all of Asia Minor and parts of Europe. Their religion was Islam, but as they conquered further East and West they assimilated new cultures and traditions. The reign of Sultan Süleyman in the 1500s was the start of a golden age for the Ottoman Empire, where art, culture and cuisine flourished. Taking influence from Anatolia, Europe, the Balkans, the Middle East and North Africa, Ottoman cuisine evolved and was refined. At its peak, during the 18th and 19th centuries, the palaces of Istanbul (then called Constantinople) set a new standard in lavish food. The kitchens of the Topkapi Palace housed 1,300 chefs, who cooked regular feasts for the sultans and their guests. They enjoyed lamb stews flavoured with paprika and walnuts, roasted pigeon, *pilav* with fruit and nuts, boreks, stuffed pepper *dolma*, spicy kebabs and smooth, milky puddings.

Istanbul was the centre of the world for an empire that spanned three continents. Trade was ruthlessly controlled and exotic ingredients flowed along the Silk Road. Hungry Ottomans, ever keen to impress, absorbed what they could into their cuisine. Today, Turkish cuisine has not forgotten any of this and the fertile country is blessed with incredible produce. The food is regional, seasonal and steeped in history. As you explore you will start to notice how the food varies from region to region, but also that firm favourites like kebabs, breads and *baklava* are enjoyed everywhere.

the regions

The Black Sea

In the beautiful Black Sea region, the people love cooking with butter, which you'll find used over and over again in the local recipes. Tea, corn, hazelnuts and saffron are grown here, and the locals fish in the dark waters of the Black Sea for *hamsi* – a silvery little anchovy that is consumed in vast quantities and loved all over the country.

Murat and I have friends and family all over Turkey, but home is Samsun, a sleepy town on the Black Sea where we go to stay with his mother, Tülay. We have had so many happy times sitting around her kitchen table eating, but my favourite meal has to be her classic Black Sea breakfast. She sets the table with plates of cucumber, sliced tomato, parsley, cheese and bread. Jam and honey are brought out and we brew tea in her magnificent Turkish teapot. As we start picking at the food, she will prepare *menemen* with mince – I love this recipe so much that I have included it in this book (see page 29). As we feast, different family members drop in to eat and share their news. The meal meanders for hours, *baklava* appears and the tea never stops flowing.

Central Anatolia

The Central Anatolian region of Turkey is home to immense plains, crystal-clear lakes and sleepy hill villages. This region was once known as the breadbasket of the world and wheat still plays a huge role in Turkey today. Soft white bread is served with every meal and the snack food of Turkey is all wheat based – *pide* (a boat-shaped pizza), *gözleme* (a folded and stuffed flatbread), *lahmacun* (a Turkish pizza) and borek (a stuffed pastry). The best place to eat these satisfying snacks is in the town of Konya. Originally established on a trade route, Konya became a cultural centre where great scholars, mystics and poets gathered in the 13th century. Today, the city retains much of this historical charm. The buildings in the old centre are still built of wood and house some of the best tea shops in Turkey, where you can put your feet up with a hot chai and tuck into a feast of local snacks.

My favourite teahouse is Pharmacy Café. Here you can watch the women sitting on the floor preparing the pastry to make their *gözleme* as you sample everything on the menu. The pastry is rolled into a circle and stuffed with lamb and cheese, then folded and cooked

on a hot stone plate, which gives it a smoky finish. They also make an incredible borek, another pastry that is stuffed with cheese, meat or spinach and baked with butter. It looks a little like a lasagne and is served in small square pieces with tea.

The Konya *pide* is really special. It is larger than the *pide* found elsewhere in Turkey and made with little chunks of lamb. The *pide* is sliced up and served with lemon wedges and parsley. This style of snack food is found all over Turkey and is loved by all ages. I have included a whole section dedicated to *pide* (see pages 62–75). Traditionally, you would eat them at a *pide* salon, cooked until crispy in a huge wood-fired oven. But if you get your oven really hot, you can make a fantastic version at home.

Marmara

Marmara, in the north-west of Turkey, is home to the cities of Istanbul and Bursa. The locals are blessed with fertile lands and seafood is caught in abundance from the Black Sea and Sea of Marmara. Istanbul, the capital city, is a melting pot of food from different cultures, religions and times. The extravagant recipes from the ancient sultans' kitchens are still prepared, and locals enjoy fabulous fusion food from the Greeks, Jews and Armenians.

Turkey is the home of the kebab, and my first destination when I land in Istanbul is Zübeyir, a restaurant where I will order an Adana Kebab (see page 90), no matter what time of day or night it is. Kebab culture is actually strongest in eastern Turkey (see right), where they love cooking meat over charcoal, and they have perfected the art over centuries.

The city of Bursa is the home of the Iskender Kebab, one of my favourite Turkish dishes, made with succulent lamb, served on soft bread and covered in yogurt and tomato sauce. It is traditional yet extravagant and I have a stripped-back recipe that you will love (see page 95).

All around this city, chestnuts grow in abundance, and in this area the locals use them in place of pistachios and almonds. You can also find chestnut kebabs sold on the roadside, as well as candied chestnuts and *pilav* adorned with these savoury nuts.

South-eastern Anatolia and East Anatolia

Together, these two vast regions make up East Turkey, cold and unforgiving in the winter and formidably hot in the summer. The food is meat-heavy and rich. The people of this area cook with lots of butter and animal fat, and eat a lot of pulses and bulgur wheat.

My first visit to the eastern side of the country was to the dusty town of Gaziantep, which is famous all over Turkey for kebabs, pistachios and *baklava*. I have dedicated a whole chapter to kebabs based on what I learned there, with traditional meat kebabs like the spicy Adana kebab and the more refined *Ali Nazik* kebab (see page 92).

Just outside Gaziantep lie the local pistachio farms. The gnarled old pistachio trees grow out of the scorched red earth and beautiful pastel pink pistachios hang heavily from the tops. At harvest, large tarpaulin mats are laid under the trees, and young lads climb to the tops of the trees and vigorously shake their branches. The pistachios rain down and are gathered up to be sorted and sold at markets around the city.

In the local *baklava* factories, shards of the bright green nuts are showered into great tins lined with pastry. A generous amount of melted butter is poured in and the *baklava* is baked in wood-fired ovens. Once golden and crispy, boiling hot sugar syrup is poured over the top and the *baklava* is left to firm up. Because *baklava* is a very labour-intensive dish, most people in Turkey buy it ready-made rather than making it at home. I have, though, included a really quick *baklava* recipe that uses shop-bought pastry, walnuts and honey (see page 218). It is very easy to make and tastes just as good as the real thing, especially with hot Turkish tea. Traditionally, you should eat this type of *baklava* upside down, so that you get the full sugary effect on your palate and the perfect crunch from the pastry, but upside down or not, it tastes divine.

Aegean and Mediterranean

Western Turkey has a much more Mediterranean mindset when it comes to eating. Here, the food is fresh and light, using lots of herbs and seafood. They cook with plenty of olive oil and love eating fresh fruit. The two regions have subtle differences: goat is used more in the Mediterranean region, and in the Aegean region they make the most of the abundance of wild herbs and flowers that are native to this area.

One of my favourite places in this part of Turkey is the sleepy stone village of Alaçati, just south of the city of Izmir on the Aegean coast. Purple and pink bougainvillea spill over the top of the pale stone houses and out into the cobbled streets of this charming place. It smells of wild herbs and lemons and, for such a small village, it is packed with bustling *balik* (fish) restaurants serving chilled *meze*, calamari, grilled octopus and fried fish. The food scene is also quite refined and we have discovered some excellent modern Turkish restaurants serving light Eastern-Med-meets-Turkish food. Our great friend Gökçen lives here. He is a famous chef in Turkey and knows the Aegean cuisine like no one else. Last time we visited, he made us a light lunch of zingy aubergine salad, samphire and grilled fish with lemon and rocket. We ate sitting at a table on the cobbled street outside his stunning stone house. It was a sublime meal and a perfect showcase for the light, fresh cuisine of this region of Turkey.

With so many wonderful regions and food so deeply steeped in culture and history, it is no wonder that I have been so inspired by the cuisine of this magnificent country. The recipes that I have put together in this book are my favourite Turkish dishes to make at home – some classic regional recipes, others old Ottoman fare and a few with a deliciously modern twist. I hope you will enjoy them all. As they say in Turkish, *serefe* – cheers!

essential ingredients

Turkish cuisine is really simple and they love to celebrate clean flavours.

Whether it's aubergine, lamb or fish, the main ingredient should always be the star of the show.

Turkish kitchens are full of fresh vegetables, fruit and herbs. Meat is bought from the local butcher and fresh bread from the baker. Cupboards are packed with spices, rice, grains and nuts. Cheese is eaten regularly and tea and coffee are kept in huge quantities to drink throughout the day. Below, I have listed some of the most commonly used Turkish ingredients, and suggested substitutes for those that are harder to get hold of.

SPICES

Spices are used in lots of Turkish recipes, both sweet and savoury. These are the essentials:

* Cumin
An earthy spice that is used ground to give a musty flavour to a variety of savoury dishes. The taste is quite subtle so you can afford to be generous with this spice.

* Cinnamon
Naturally sweet, cinnamon is used to flavour stews, *pilav* and many sweet dishes in Turkish cooking. You can find wonderful rolled cinnamon sticks and ultra-fine, ground cinnamon, which is what I use in this book.

* Saffron
Picked from purple crocus flowers, this fragrant spice imparts a vibrant yellow colour and an incredible pungent aroma. Good-quality saffron is expensive, but a little pinch goes a long way.

* Sumac
This ground red berry has a wonderfully sour tang and is used in salads, meat dishes and kebabs to add an extra hit of flavour.

* Allspice
As the name suggests, allspice really does have a flavour that is hard to define, but it adds a sensational background note that works beautifully in rice dishes and stews.

* Pul biber – Turkish pepper flakes
Made from dried red pepper, these flakes have a smoky taste and a mild piquant quality. They are typically Turkish and used in lots of recipes, as well as being a condiment to add to your food at the table. You can find *pul biber* in good-quality Turkish grocery stores or online. If you can't find them, use a little smoked paprika with a pinch of chilli flakes, or a spicy smoked paprika.

* Black pepper
This ancient spice is used generously in Turkish cooking to add favour and warmth. Be generous and make sure that you use freshly ground black pepper so that you get the best taste.

CURED MEATS

Cured meats are used to add an instant meaty hit to many dishes, from eggs to white beans.

* Sujuk
Sujuk (traditionally spelt '*sucuk*') is a cured sausage made from beef. It is smoky and can be spicy. You can find it in Turkish grocery stores or online. It has a waxy skin that is best removed. As it is cured, it cooks very quickly. If you can't get *sujuk*, use a cured beef or, if you eat pork, chorizo.

* Turkish pastrami
This smoky ingredient is used with eggs and generously on pide. It has a slightly chewy texture and a really smoky flavour. You can find it in Turkish grocery stores. If you can't get hold of Turkish pastrami, use a really good-quality dried beef salami or Parma ham, if you eat pork.

FRUIT

Fresh fruit is eaten after most meals and some fruits are also used in cooking.

* Lemons
One of the main cooking ingredients in so many Turkish dishes. It is always worth having piles of lemons around, and if you find yourself with any leftovers, mix the juice with water and a little sugar to make a glass of refreshing lemon water.

* Pomegranates

These are squeezed on street corners for juice and the seeds are used to add a sweet tang to salads, desserts and meat dishes.

* Dried figs, apricots and dates

As well as being served with breakfast, these are also used in lots of the older Ottoman dishes to add a mild sweetness.

FRESH VEGETABLES

Bought from local markets, great mounds of fresh vegetables are kept in every Turkish kitchen.

* Onions and garlic

The base of so many great dishes, onions and garlic are used in most recipes in Turkey. Slow-cooked onions and garlic start all the great stews off and they love using sweet raw onions, finely sliced in salads and as a side dish to have with grilled meats.

* Tomatoes

Juicy, ripe tomatoes are loved all over Turkey and most people will serve sliced tomatoes for breakfast. They also make the sauce for many incredible stews and add a beautiful bright red colour to numerous Turkish salads.

* Aubergines

Turkish people love eating aubergines and they have hundreds of ways to use this fabulous vegetable, from mashed to roasted and grilled. They are often scorched until almost black over a flame in order to give the flesh a wonderful smoky flavour.

* Turkish green peppers

These look like long, slightly twisted green chillies. But they have a very mild heat and a sweeter flavour than the green peppers we know. If you can't find them in your local Turkish or Middle-Eastern grocer, use red peppers instead.

CHEESES

Cheese is whipped out for breakfast, slipped into lunch and used as a topping for a huge variety of breads and pastries. Each region has a wonderful variety of local cheeses, which are very hard to get abroad. I have given supermarket-friendly version in my recipes that will work just as well.

* Beyaz peynir

A crumbly, feta-like cheese that is milky white and medium soft. It is great in salads.

* Kaşar

This is a hard cheese that has a wonderful melting quality. It is not too oily, so perfect when hot. Cheddar is similar and works just as well.

* Erzurum tulum peyniri

I love this soft, creamy cheese that is great in the morning with honey. It is perfect to fold into anything sweet. Ricotta is the best substitute.

* Lor peyniri

This soft, stringy cheese is ideal for ripping over salads or melting. It is slightly rubbery, so stays together when melted. Mozzarella is the best substitute.

YOGURT

Thick, creamy yogurt is made all over Turkey and served with most meals. Greek yogurt is similar and easy to source. Yogurt is watered down to make a drink call *ayran* and hung up in muslin to make a thicker version called *labnah* that is used to make *meze* dips.

BREAD, RICE AND GRAINS

These form the backbone of Turkish cooking. Bread is served with everything, and on every street corner you can buy *simit*, a doughy sesame-covered pretzel, to eat as breakfast on the go. You can find amazing Turkish breads in a Turkish or Middle Eastern shop, but if you don't have one nearby use the freshest bread you can find. *Pilavs* can be lavish or simply prepared with butter and orzo. I use basmati rice when I cook mine at home. Turkish cooks use lots of pearl barley, couscous and bulgur. They have a real respect for wholegrains and use the natural nuttiness to their advantage.

TEA AND COFFEE

Turkish *çay* (tea) is drunk throughout the day, served black with sugar on the side. It is brewed in what looks like two teapots stacked on top of each other. The idea is that you brew tea in the bottom one and keep boiling water in the top one. You add a little of the strong black tea to your cup and top it up with the hot water to your preferred strength. Thick black Turkish coffee has an intense chocolatey flavour and is served in espresso cups. It is not filtered, so you have to leave the residue at the bottom – or if you want to get really Turkish, flip the finished cup over into the saucer, tap it and wait 5 minutes, then try to read your fortune!

HERBS

Herbs are hugely important in Turkish cooking and are grown all over the country.

* Parsley, mint and dill

This classic trio of fresh herbs is used in so many Turkish dishes. Parsley is adored, and they often serve plates of fresh parsley at meal times for you to roll up and eat, or add to your food as you like. It a very healthy herb, so it's great to eat as often as you can.

* Mint, oregano and thyme

These herbs are dried in the summer to use throughout the year to flavour stews, *köftes* and kebabs. Dried mint is added to melted butter and used as a temper for soups, stews and *manti*, a traditional Turkish ravioli.

NUTS

Nuts are grown all over Turkey and they play an important part in the diet.

* Walnuts

These are served with breakfast and also enrich many sweet and savoury dishes.

* Almonds

Turkish people love using almonds in desserts, ground or whole, and since the Ottoman times, toasted almonds have adorned bejewelled *pilavs*.

* Pistachios

Grown in the south-east of Turkey, pistachios are used to flavour desserts and elaborate rice dishes. The variety they have in Turkey is madly green in colour and if you can find similar in a good Middle-Eastern or Turkish shop, they are a beautiful ingredient to use.

OLIVES AND OLIVE OIL

Turkey has been growing olives and producing oil for centuries. Olives are served with most meals and olive oil used to dress cooked vegetables and salads.

STORECUPBOARD

Every Turkish household will keep these essentials.

* Pomegranate molasses

A sticky, tangy fruity molasses that is made from concentrated pomegranate juice. It is used to dress salads, and add a tangy hit to stews or kebabs.

* Honey

Turkey is blessed with incredible fragrant honey. During summer, you can find great slabs of honeycomb in the markets. It is eaten at breakfast and used to flavour desserts. I like to keep a jar of best-quality lavender honey in the cupboard for when I need it.

* Red pepper paste

Every home keeps this thick, smoky, concentrated red pepper paste. It is used very liberally in Turkish cooking and you can find it in all good Turkish or Middle-Eastern grocers.

* Tomato purée

We are more familiar with this ingredient, which is used in so many classic Turkish recipes to add an instant tomato hit.

* Pickles

Stored in massive plastic tubs, pickles are served as a side to most meals. They can be anything from peppers to carrots and even cabbage.

1
breakfast

A traditional Turkish breakfast is the biggest meal of the day.

It is a long and lazy affair, but is eaten on small plates and with small cutlery in order to avoid over-eating. Breakfast is a central part of Turkish family life. Many Turks who live abroad will still get up early in their adopted countries and indulge in this morning ritual, filling their tables with a delicious spread. Dozens of little plates are laid out, piled high with juicy tomatoes sliced up and covered in olive oil, cucumbers, black olives, fresh parsley, walnuts, cheeses, honey, jam and bread. These are enjoyed with black tea, thick Turkish coffee and glasses of freshly squeezed orange juice. Eggs are also served, either plainly fried, fried with a Turkish salami called *sujuk*, or as *menemen*, scrambled eggs with tomatoes, green peppers and meat (see page 29).

Turkey is a vast country, and so breakfast varies from region to region. On the coast, lots of fresh fruit is served, while in Anatolia they love eating buttery *gözleme*, rustic flatbreads stuffed with meat and cheese and cooked on a large, flat, stone plate. On the huge plains of south-east Turkey they love a sweet pastry called *katmer* (see page 234), which is made from thin layers of pastry stuffed with pistachios and *kaymak* (Turkish clotted cream), served with big bowls of the bright red cherries that grow all over this region. Further north, towards the Black Sea, the famous anchovy, or *hamsi*, is made into a *pide* using cornflour and then fried. It is fabulous served with a dollop of thick, spicy tomato salsa.

The breakfast in Van, in Southeast Anatolia, is truly special. Surrounded by huge mountains, the locals of this magical city on Lake Van tuck into an enormous breakfast of *murtuga*, a thick paste made from flour, eggs and butter, served with yogurt, buttery fried eggs and fresh, herby cheeses.

The breakfast recipes that follow are authentic, inspired by all these regions, but are also easy make. To achieve a real Turkish experience, cook a savoury dish and serve it with cucumber, tomatoes and a soft white cheese... oh, and make sure there is a sweet dish to follow.

Black Sea Pancake

This heavenly pancake is a classic Black Sea breakfast. Fresh herbs and spring greens are finely chopped and mixed into a lovely light batter. I learnt this recipe from my friend Saliha, who lives with her family in a beautiful house high in the hills overlooking the town of Trabzon and the dark waters of the Black Sea. She serves these pancakes with a tangy salad of chopped parsley and onions covered in olive oil and lemon juice. You can use any greens you like, but baby spinach works very well.

120g plain flour
150ml full-fat milk
4 eggs
80g spring greens (baby spinach is great)
a handful of chopped flat-leaf parsley leaves
3 spring onions, finely chopped
3 tablespoons olive oil
sea salt

Makes 2 large pancakes

1. Tip the flour into a mixing bowl, add the milk and whisk to a smooth batter. Add the eggs and a pinch of salt and whisk together.

2. Stir the greens, parsley and spring onions into the batter.

3. Heat the oil in a large non-stick frying pan over a medium–high heat. Pour in half of the batter and spread out in an even layer. Make a few holes in the pancake using a fork and tilt the pan slightly from side to side to fill the holes with the uncooked batter to get a really even layer. Cook for 2–2½ minutes on each side until lightly golden. Repeat with the remaining batter and serve immediately.

Butter Beans with *Sujuk*

Sujuk is a smoked Turkish sausage made from beef. Being a Muslim country, the Turkish don't eat pork, although it can occasionally be found in Istanbul. However, they have perfected the art of curing beef so that they have incredible smoky, spicy *sujuk* and wonderful silky beef *pastirma*, or pastrami, that is delicious with eggs in the morning, or on a *pide*. You can find *sujuk* in Turkish food shops, or, if you eat pork, you can just use a mild chorizo instead.

Traditionally served as a *meze* dish, these beans also make the perfect brunch. The sauce becomes rich and thick as it cooks, taking on the flavour of the fried *sujuk*. This is ideal served with crusty bread and, if you want to go all out, a poached egg on top.

2 tablespoons olive oil
200g *sujuk* (or mild chorizo), sliced into half moons
1 red onion, finely chopped
1 garlic clove, finely chopped
2 Turkish green peppers, deseeded and finely chopped
4 tomatoes, skinned and finely chopped
2 x 400g tins butter beans, drained and rinsed
½ teaspoon Turkish pepper flakes
½ teaspoon ground cumin
1½ tablespoons tomato purée
200ml boiling water
a handful of finely chopped flat-leaf parsley leaves
sea salt and freshly ground black pepper
crusty bread, to serve

Serves 4

1. Heat the oil in a frying pan over a medium heat and add the *sujuk*. Cook for 1½–2 minutes on each side until golden. Remove from the pan and set to one side.

2. Reheat the pan over a medium heat and add the onion. Cook, stirring occasionally, for 3–4 minutes until soft. Add the garlic and green peppers and continue to cook, stirring occasionally, for 2–3 minutes until soft. Stir in the tomatoes, butter beans, Turkish pepper flakes, cumin, tomato purée and a good pinch of salt and black pepper. Pour in the boiling water, mix well, cover and reduce the heat to low. Simmer for 10 minutes.

3. Return the *sujuk* to the pan and mix together. Turn the heat up a little until bubbling, then cook, stirring occasionally, for 12–15 minutes, or until the sauce is lovely and thick. Scatter over the parsley and serve immediately with crusty bread.

Yumurtali Ekmek – Turkish-style French Toast

Although I have described it as French Toast, *Yumurtali Ekmek* is actually a very traditional Turkish breakfast recipe that is served all over the country. Like most things in Turkey, it has been given a spicy sprinkling to enhance it, with Turkish pepper flakes (see page 15), cumin and dried mint adding plenty of flavour. This recipe traditionally calls for *beyaz peyniri*, or 'white cheese'. This is essentially a feta cheese that the Turkish eat at breakfast. It melts over the 'Turkish toast' and adds an extra savoury dimension.

2 eggs
60ml full-fat milk
½ teaspoon Turkish pepper flakes
½ teaspoon ground cumin
½ teaspoon dried mint
2 thick slices of white bread
1½ tablespoons butter
30g feta cheese
sea salt

Serves 2

1. Crack the eggs into a shallow dish and add the milk, Turkish pepper flakes, cumin and mint. Season with salt and whisk together.
Dunk the bread slices into the egg mixture and leave for 30 seconds.
Flip over, then leave for a couple of minutes to absorb all the egg.

2. Melt the butter in a large frying pan over a medium heat.
Add the bread and cook for 2–2½ minutes on each side until golden.
Serve the bread immediately with feta crumbled over the top.

Ispanaklı Yumurta – Baked Eggs with Spinach

This dish is inspired by the classic Turkish *ispanaklı yumurta*, a hearty breakfast that is eaten across Turkey. Not only is this brilliant breakfast healthy, it also tastes divine. As in the traditional recipe, I use smoky Turkish pepper flakes. They add just the right kick to wake you up in the morning, and the hint of spice from the cumin gives an extra hit of flavour.

2 tablespoons olive oil
1 onion, finely chopped
1 garlic clove, finely chopped
520g baby spinach
1 teaspoon Turkish pepper flakes
½ teaspoon ground cumin
4 eggs
sea salt and freshly ground black pepper

Serves 4

1. Preheat the oven to 180°C/gas mark 4. Heat the oil in a large ovenproof frying pan over a high heat. Add the onion and fry for 2–3 minutes until just golden. Add the garlic and cook for 10 seconds until fragrant.

2. Add the spinach in three batches and fry each batch for 2–2½ minutes, tipping out any excess moisture as you go. Once you have fried the last batch, sprinkle in the Turkish pepper flakes, cumin and a good pinch of salt and black pepper. Fry for a further minute, or until any excess moisture has gone.

3. Make four wells in the spinach using the back of a spoon and crack in the eggs. Pop the pan in the oven for 4–5 minutes, or until the egg whites are just set and the yolks still gloriously runny. Serve immediately.

Poached Eggs, Yogurt and Avocado

The classic Turkish egg dish, *çilbir*, comes knee-deep in yogurt and swimming in a naughty (but oh so nice) chilli butter. This twist on the traditional recipe goes easy on both the butter and yogurt, instead bringing in creamy avocado. The different textures, temperatures and colours all work together beautifully to help set you up for the day. As in the traditional dish, the Turkish pepper flakes are added to the melted butter so that the flavours and deep red colour of the spice bleed out and run all over the finished dish.

2 eggs
2 slices of wholemeal bread
1½ tablespoons butter
½ teaspoon Turkish
pepper flakes
2 avocados
juice of ½ lemon
100g Greek yogurt
sea salt and freshly ground
black pepper

Serves 2

1. Poach the eggs in boiling water for 3–4 minutes until they are set and the yolks are beautifully runny.

2. Meanwhile, toast the bread, and melt the butter in a small pan over a medium heat for 2–3 minutes until bubbling. Add the Turkish pepper flakes to the butter, then take the pan off the heat.

3. Scoop the avocado flesh out into a mixing bowl. Pour in the lemon juice and season with salt and black pepper. Mash together and spread generously onto the toast.

4. Tip the yogurt into a mixing bowl and add 2 tablespoons of cold water. Season with a good pinch of salt and mix together to loosen.

5. To serve, divide the toast between two serving plates and top each slice with a poached egg. Spoon over the yogurt and drizzle over the melted butter. Serve immediately.

Mince *Menemen*

Ask any Turkish person what they eat for breakfast each week and they will undoubtedly say they eat *menemen* at least twice. Once you have tried it, you will see why. Tomatoes, peppers and onions are cooked slowly and then eggs are whisked in and gently scrambled. This version is inspired by *kıymalı menemen*, a traditional dish made with lamb mince. The meat melts into the eggs, giving masses of extra flavour. With a large coffee, this is the ultimate hangover breakfast... just in case you might be in need.

2 tablespoons butter
1 onion, finely chopped
6 Turkish green peppers, deseeded and finely sliced
220g lamb mince
3 tomatoes, skinned and roughly chopped
1 teaspoon Turkish pepper flakes
1 teaspoon freshly ground black pepper
½ teaspoon ground cumin
4 eggs
sea salt

Serves 4

1. Heat a large frying pan over a medium heat and melt the butter. Add the onion and fry for 2 minutes until translucent. Stir in the peppers and lamb mince and fry for 4–5 minutes, or until the meat has browned.

2. Tip in the tomatoes, Turkish pepper flakes, black pepper, cumin and a good pinch of salt. Mix together thoroughly. Reduce the heat to low, cover and cook, stirring occasionally, for 6–7 minutes, or until the tomatoes have broken down.

3. Push the back of a spoon into the mix to make four wells and crack in the eggs. Cover, reduce the heat to low and cook for 6–7 minutes, or until the eggs are just set. Serve immediately with loads of bread and Turkish *çay* tea.

Village Pancakes
with Honey and Clotted Cream

Served in the beautiful stone village of Alaçati on the Aegean coast, these delicate pancakes are the perfect breakfast for anyone with a sweet tooth. The pillowy light pancakes use soft-peak egg whites to keep them extra fluffy and are served with thick *süt kaymak* or clotted cream and a lovely local honeycomb from the surrounding lavender-covered hills. If you can't find honeycomb, get a really good runny lavender honey from the supermarket.

2 eggs, separated
220g plain flour
1 teaspoon baking powder
a pinch of salt
2 teaspoons caster sugar
300ml full-fat milk
50g butter, melted and slighlty cooled, plus a little extra for frying

To serve
jam of your choice
clotted cream
runny honey or honeycomb

Serves 2

1. Whisk the egg whites into soft peaks.

2. Combine the flour, baking powder, salt and sugar in a separate large mixing bowl. Make a well in the centre and add the egg yolks. Start whisking together and pour in the milk, a little at a time, until it is all incorporated into the batter. Pour in the melted butter and mix together. Gently fold in the egg whites.

3. Heat a small knob of butter in a large non-stick frying pan and ladle in a table tennis ball-sized portion of the batter. Cook for a minute on each side until golden. Once bubbles appear in the middle of the pancake, it's time to flip it over. Transfer to a serving plate and repeat with the remaining batter to make 6–8 pancakes.

4. Serve the pancakes in stacks topped with your favourite jam, clotted cream and some honeycomb or a drizzle of honey.

Tahin *Pekmez* Toast

Pekmez and tahini is traditionally a very Anatolian dish, but the recipe has been picked up by most of western Turkey. French toast is covered in a rich sauce made from tahini and Turkish grape molasses, which has the most unbelievable summery sweet flavour. It is made during the autumn in the villages of the grape-growing regions of Turkey. The grapes are trampled and then cooked for hours. The mixture is filtered several times during the process to ensure a really pure final product. You can find this molasses in Turkish food shops, but if you can't get hold of any, just use a high-quality runny honey and a tiny squeeze of lemon.

2 eggs
60ml full-fat milk
2 thick slices of white bread
1½ tablespoons butter
2 tablespoons tahini paste
2 tablespoons Turkish grape molasses

Serves 2

1. Crack the eggs into a shallow dish and add the milk. Whisk together. Dunk the bread slices into the egg mixture and leave for 30 seconds. Flip over, then leave for a couple of minutes to absorb all the egg.

2. Melt the butter in a large frying pan over a medium heat. Add the bread and cook for 2–2½ minutes on each side until golden.

3. Meanwhile, mix the tahini and molasses together in a small bowl with 3 tablespoons of cold water. It will go dry at first, but keep mixing and it will relax into a smooth sauce.

4. To serve, divide the French toast between two plates, drizzle over the tahini sauce and serve immediately.

Pomegranate Jam

I first tasted this jam one morning when I was sitting with my friends Sebahat and Osman in the shade under an ancient fig tree in their beautiful courtyard in Alaçati. At the end of a true Turkish feast of a breakfast, we were sipping çay (tea) when Osman produced a magnificent array of homemade jams: lemon, mandarin and vibrant pink pomegranate jam. Each one was made with seasonal fruit and natural apple pectin, which sets the jam. The pomegranate was my favourite and I managed to persuade Osman to part with his recipe. Every time I make this glorious fruit jam the smell reminds me of their wonderful company and beautiful home.

5 Granny Smith apples, chopped into 2.5cm cubes, pips in and skin on, stalks removed
7 pomegranates
460g caster sugar
juice of 1 lemon

To sterilise a jam jar, take a clean jar that has just been washed and fill it right to the top with just-boiled water from a kettle. Cover with the lid and leave for 3–5 minutes. Pour out the water and let the jar cool for a few seconds, then use immediately.

Makes 1 x 340g jar

1. Start by making the pectin. Put the apples into a saucepan and pour over 1.25l of just boiled water. Bring to the boil over a high heat and cook for 10 minutes. Reduce the heat to medium and boil gently for a further 15 minutes. Remove the fruit from the heat and leave to cool for about half an hour. Tip into a fine sieve and strain into a bowl, reserving the cooking water. Using the back of a spoon, gently push the apples to get out all the pectin for the jam. Discard the apples and keep the pectin water.

2. Using an old fashioned orange squeezer, squeeze 6 of the pomegranates, and sieve the juice with a fine sieve to remove any bits.

3. Pour the sugar, lemon juice, pomegranate juice and apple pectin water into a heavy casserole dish. Bring to the boil over a high heat and remove any scum from the surface with a metal spoon. Reduce the heat to low and cook gently for 2–3 hours, continuing to remove any scum as you go, or until the jam has reduced by three quarters and is really thick. To test when it's ready, put a drop of jam onto a side plate and leave it to cool for a few seconds. It should remain in a blob and not run. You can taste the jam and add some more lemon juice if you think it's too sweet. Remove from the heat and leave to cool for 30 minutes.

4. Meanwhile, remove the seeds from the last pomegranate. Add to the cooled jam and mix well. Pour into a sterilised jam jar and leave to cool for 24 hours before serving with fresh bread and lots of butter. Once opened, this jam will keep for up to 2 weeks in the fridge.

2

meze

For me, *meze* is truly Turkish.

It is a selection of dishes that are served at the start of a meal, alongside plenty of soft white bread. The conversation flows and these tempting small bites lead you into what you know is going to be a fabulous long dinner. Everyone stays up for hours, late into the warm evenings, enjoying the food and company. It is a very social way to eat.

The word *meze* is believed to come from the Persian *mazze*, meaning taste or snack. These *mazze* dishes were served during the Ottoman Empire as a starter to a grand meal or, more excitingly, as an appetiser that was served with alcohol at the local tavern, or *meyhane*.

Traditionally, men would gather in their nearest *meyhane* for a long evening of *raki*, the Turkish national drink, and endless *meze* dishes. Despite being a Muslim country, Turkey has always had alcohol as part of its culture, with incredible old wines and *raki*.

Made from molasses, this clear aniseed drink is served neat or chilled over ice, turning a milky white colour as it is poured.

There are so many *meze* dishes served across Turkey: smoked aubergine dip; *cacik*, made from yogurt and cucumber; a spicy walnut paste called *muhammara*; a vibrant chilli salad called *acılı ezme* (see page 40); chopped aubergine salads; fava bean paste; courgette fritters; fried liver; *köfte*; and borek.

In Turkish culture, *meze* changes depending on the main course. If you're having fish as a main dish, the typical *meze* is samphire, aubergines with yogurt, octopus salad, calamari or fava beans. But if a kebab is being served, the *meze* changes to a more spicy eastern fare of *acılı ezme*, *içli köfte* and *haydari*. However you decide to eat your *meze*, make sure you make several dishes and serve with good bread and great company.

Acılı Ezme – Chilli Salad

Acılı ezme is a classic *meze* dish that is served at the start of meals throughout Turkey, with piles of freshly baked bread and *cacik*, a cooling yogurt and cucumber dip. This salad is packed with fresh herbs, Turkish peppers and tomatoes in a tangy pomegranate dressing, giving it fresh, spicy flavours and a juicy texture. I love *acılı ezme* any time, but my real weakness is having this vibrant salad with a chargrilled lamb kebab. The freshness of the salad works so well with the smoky meat, and the delicious juices can be soaked up with lots of soft flatbread.

3 tomatoes, skinned, deseeded and finely chopped
3 Turkish green peppers, deseeded and finely chopped
4 handfuls of finely chopped flat-leaf parsley leaves
2 handfuls of finely chopped mint leaves
1 teaspoon sumac
1 ½ teaspoons Turkish pepper flakes
juice of ½ lemon
2 tablespoons pomegranate molasses (see page 17)
1 tablespoon extra virgin olive oil, for drizzling
sea salt

Serves 4

1. Put the tomatoes, green peppers, herbs, sumac, Turkish pepper flakes, lemon juice, pomegranate molasses and a good pinch of salt into a mixing bowl. Mix together really well and tip onto a serving dish.

2. Drizzle over the olive oil and serve immediately.

Paçanga Börēgi – Cheese and Pastrami Borek

This delicious melted cheese and pastrami borek is one of my favourite mid-afternoon snacks. Originally, it would have been the recipe that used up leftovers; any extra cheese, meat and vegetables would be put into a borek and served with *raki*. Like so many recipes, *paçanga börēgi* has been refined to a simple dish with butter, cheese and pastrami. The cheese melts inside the pastry and the pastrami adds a perfect hit of savouriness. The recipe uses Turkish pastrami, which has a strong, salty flavour. You can find this in Turkish food shops, otherwise use a good pastrami from your local supermarket.

4 sheets of filo pastry
35g butter, melted
4 slices of Turkish pastrami
120g *kaşar* or Cheddar cheese
1 egg, beaten

Makes 4

1. Preheat the oven to 180°C/gas mark 4. Line a baking sheet with baking paper. Lay a sheet of filo pastry onto a chopping board with the long edges at the sides and the shorter edges at the top and bottom. Brush all over with melted butter. Lay a slice of pastrami about 5cm from the bottom of the filo pastry sheet and top with a quarter of the cheese. Fold the long edges of pastry inwards by about 2cm on each side, then fold over the bottom 5cm of pastry so that it covers the pastrami. Working from the bottom, roll the pastry up so it looks like a sausage roll. Place onto the baking tray and repeat with the rest of the pastry and filling.

2. Brush the tops of the borek with beaten egg and bake for 15–18 minutes until golden and crispy. Serve immediately.

M's Basil Tabbouleh

My partner, Murat, makes his basil tabbouleh for me whenever we have a barbecue – it's his spin on the classic Middle Eastern tabbouleh that is prepared throughout Turkey as a *meze* dish. The trick to making the perfect tabbouleh is to hand chop the herbs and vegetables really finely, so that when they are dressed and the flavours mix together, the juices get soaked up by the bulgur. The addition of basil is brilliant – it makes the tabbouleh more fragrant and a little sweeter, and I love that contrast against the tangy dressing.

60g bulgur wheat
100ml boiling water
4 handfuls of finely chopped
flat-leaf parsley leaves
2 handfuls of finely chopped
mint leaves
2 handfuls of finely chopped
basil leaves
1 red onion, finely chopped
2 tomatoes, peeled, deseeded
and finely chopped
1 garlic clove, crushed
juice of 1 lemon
3 tablespoons olive oil
2 tablespoons pomegranate
molasses
½ teaspoon sumac
sea salt and freshly ground
black pepper

Serves 4

1. Tip the bulgur wheat into a mixing bowl and pour over the boiling water. Cover with clingfilm and set to one side while you prepare the other ingredients.

2. Combine the herbs, onion, tomatoes and garlic in a large mixing bowl. Pour in the lemon juice, oil and pomegranate molasses. Season and mix together.

3. Tip the bulgur into the tabbouleh, add 2 tablespoons of cold water and mix together. Leave to stand for 10 minutes before serving so that the bulgur can absorb some of the wonderful fresh flavours. Transfer to a serving dish. Scatter over the sumac and serve immediately.

Alaçati Borek

Borek is found in different guises all over Turkey. Various types of pastry are filled with meat, vegetables, cheese or sweet fillings. Everyone loves it and has a favourite type. This recipe is a spin on the traditional *sigara böregi*, or rolled borek. Lamb, onion, parsley and spices are mixed with a soft cheese, rolled in pastry and cooked. I favour a triangle shape rather than the cigar as you can pack in more filling this way. In Turkey, the borek would be stuffed with *Erzurum tulum peyniri*, a soft creamy white cheese that has a very mild flavour. I have used ricotta cheese for this recipe as it has the same texture and flavour and is easier to come by outside of Turkey.

1 tablespoon olive oil
220g lamb mince
½ red onion, finely chopped
2 garlic cloves, crushed
a handful of finely chopped
flat-leaf parsley leaves
1 teaspoon freshly ground
black pepper
½ teaspoon Turkish
pepper flakes
250g ricotta cheese
5 sheets of filo pastry
1 egg, beaten
1 teaspoon nigella seeds
sea salt

Serves 4–6 (makes 10)

1. Heat the oil in a pan over a medium heat and fry the lamb and onion for 2–3 minutes until the lamb is just cooked through.

2. Add the garlic and fry for 10 seconds until fragrant. Remove from the heat and tip into a mixing bowl. Leave to cool for a few minutes, then add the parsley, black pepper, Turkish pepper flakes, ricotta and a good pinch of salt. Mix everything together well.

3. Preheat the oven to 180°C/gas mark 4. Take a piece of filo pastry and cut it in half so you have two rectangles. Lay one of the pieces out lengthways. Fold up the bottom right corner to form a triangle. Pull it back and place a walnut-sized piece of the filling where it will be covered by the pastry triangle. Now fold the corner back up so the triangle covers the filling, then carefully fold this triangle to the left, then down, continuing with the triangle shape. Brush the remaining filo with egg wash and fold the triangle over itself, closing the gap. Secure any excess pastry with egg wash so you have a neat triangle shape. Place on a baking sheet lined with baking paper and repeat until all the filling is used up.

4. Brush the top of the triangles with beaten egg and scatter over the nigella seeds. Bake for 15–20 minutes until golden and crispy. Leave to cool for a few minutes before serving.

Freekeh, Yogurt and Spinach Salad

This is a classic *meze* dish that comes from Izmir on the west coast of Turkey. The smoky freekeh melts into the yogurt sauce and the spicy butter brings it all together beautifully. I first ate this dish with my friend, Aysenur, who is a fabulous cook. Her mother taught her how to make this and her mother before that. Aysenur served the salad at room temperature with braised fennel *meze* and thick garlicky yogurt. If you can't find freekeh in the shops, you can substitute it for bulgur wheat and still get the same nutty flavour.

200g freekeh
2 tablespoons olive oil
1 onion, finely chopped
200g baby spinach, washed
350g Greek yogurt
a handful of finely chopped
flat-leaf parsley
juice of ½ lemon
30g butter
1 teaspoon tomato purée
1 teaspoon dried mint
½ teaspoon Turkish
pepper flakes
sea salt

Serves 4

1. Cook the freekeh according to the packet instructions in a large saucepan of boiling water. Drain, refresh under cold running water and drain again, thoroughly. Tip into a mixing bowl.

2. Meanwhile, heat the oil in a frying pan over a medium heat. Add the onion and cook, stirring occasionally, for 3–4 minutes until translucent. Add the spinach and a pinch of salt. Mix well and cook for 2–3 minutes until wilted. Leave to cool for a few minutes, then add to the freekeh.

3. Add the yogurt, parsley, lemon juice and a pinch of salt to the bowl. Mix well and tip onto a serving dish.

4. Heat the butter in a small pan over a low–medium heat until melted. Add the tomato purée, mint, Turkish pepper flakes and a pinch of salt. Mix well and remove from the heat. Leave to infuse for a minute, then pour over the salad and serve immediately.

Aubergine Salad

There are different varieties of cold aubergine salad served all over Turkey and this fresh zingy version is typical of the Mediterranean region. The aubergines take on the classic Turkish smoky flavour in the oven (you can, alternatively, cook the aubergines and peppers over a gas flame) and the whole thing is freshened up with flecks of red onion, pomegranate seeds and lots of lemon juice. This salad would be served with a selection of *meze* dishes at the start of a meal, with plenty of fresh bread and peppery olive oil.

2 aubergines
2 red peppers
3 tablespoons olive oil
½ red onion, finely chopped
1 garlic clove, crushed
2 large handfuls of finely chopped flat-leaf parsley
juice of 1½ lemons
seeds from ½ pomegranate
sea salt and freshly ground black pepper

Serves 4

1. Preheat the oven to 200°C/gas mark 6. Put the aubergines and red peppers into a mixing bowl and rub the oil all over them. Tip into a roasting dish and roast for 45–50 minutes until charred and tender. Remove from the oven and leave to cool.

2. Scrape out the aubergine flesh, discarding the skin, and finely chop into a coarse paste. Tip into a mixing bowl. Cut the tops off the red peppers and deseed them. Remove and discard the skin. Finely chop the peppers and add to the bowl with the aubergines.

3. Stir in the onion, garlic, parsley, lemon juice and a good pinch of salt and black pepper. Mix everything together well. Transfer to a serving dish and scatter over the pomegranate seeds. Serve immediately.

Charred Samphire with Lemon

The Aegean coast of Turkey is stunning: rugged rocky outcrops, long, white sandy beaches and crystal-clear, azure sea. The food of this region is fresh and light, with lots of vegetables. Samphire grows in the coves of the Aegean coast in the hot summer months and is served boiled as a simple salad at *balik* (fish) restaurants. This mouthwatering recipe is slightly different from the traditional boiled version. The samphire is griddled to give it a smoky finish, then dressed in olive oil, lemon and garlic while still warm, so that it soaks up all the flavours as it cools.

180g samphire
3 tablespoons olive oil
juice of ½ lemon
1 garlic clove, crushed

Serves 4

1. Blanch the samphire in a saucepan of boiling water for 3–4 minutes until tender. Refresh in iced water and drain.

2. Heat a griddle pan over a high heat until smoking. Meanwhile, pour the oil into a flat dish. Add the lemon juice and garlic and mix together.

3. Griddle the samphire in batches. Spread it out onto the griddle and cook for 2 minutes until a little charred and smoky. Remove from the pan and toss straight into the dressing. Repeat with remaining samphire and leave for 2 minutes to soak up the dressing. Serve immediately.

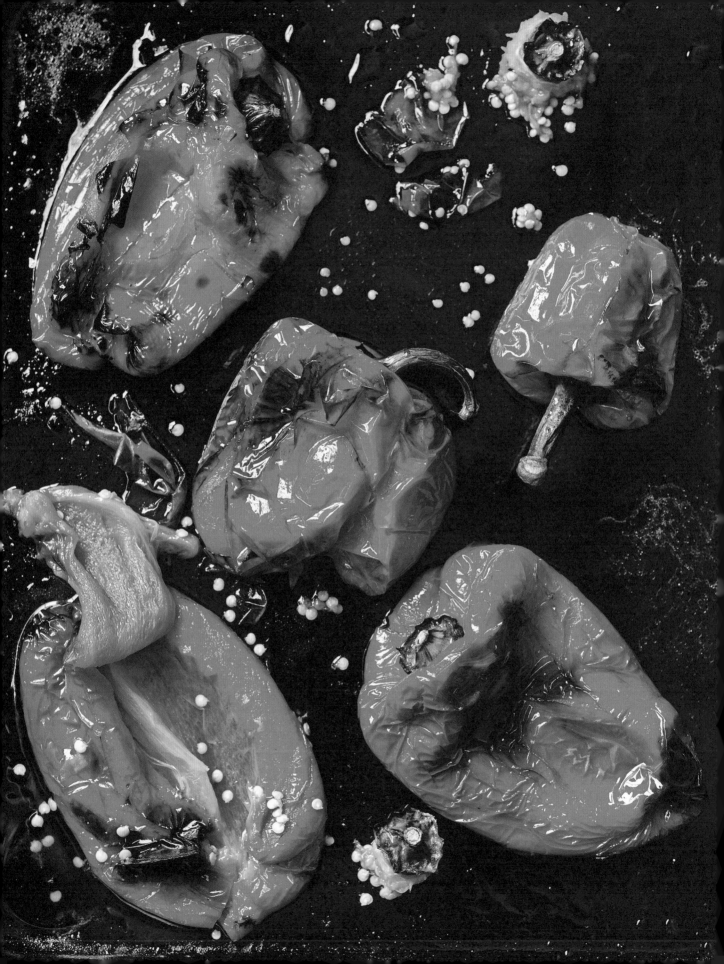

Yoğurtlu Közlenmiş Biber – Red Pepper Dip

Red pepper dip, or red pepper salad, as it is known in Turkey, is a staple *meze* dish that is served across the entire country. The cooked peppers are mixed into a smooth paste with yogurt and garlic. I have made a slightly more modern version using dill and walnuts as garnish. I love the extra flavour and texture they add to the creamy peppers. The dip works perfectly as part of a *meze* spread, along with beetroot dip, freekeh with spinach and fresh bread.

4 red peppers
2 tablespoons olive oil
180g Greek yogurt
juice of ½ lemon
1 garlic clove, crushed
½ teaspoon Turkish
pepper flakes
30g walnuts, finely chopped
a handful of finely chopped dill
sea salt and freshly ground
black pepper

Serves 4

1. Preheat the oven to 200°C/gas mark 6. Put the red peppers into a mixing bowl and add the oil. Season with salt and black pepper and mix well. Tip into a roasting dish and roast for 40–45 minutes until charred and tender, then leave to cool.

2. When cool, remove the stalks and deseed and skin the peppers. Put the flesh into a blender and add the yogurt, lemon juice, garlic and Turkish pepper flakes. Pulse to a fine paste. Check the seasoning. Transfer to a serving dish. Scatter over the walnuts and dill, and serve immediately.

Cabbage *Dolma*

Dolma was a very popular Ottoman food. Aubergines, courgettes or peppers were hollowed out and stuffed with beautifully flavoured rice, then cooked slowly to create a lavish dish perfect for the opulent dinner parties of the sultans. As well as vegetables, *dolma* extended to cabbage and vine leaves that were rolled up with a filling and cooked in the same way. Today, most Turkish households will have a stack of cabbage leaf *dolma* in the fridge for hungry visitors. They are served as a quick snack, a *meze* dish, or even as a side for a long, lazy breakfast.

14 large cabbage leaves
½ onion, finely chopped
50g rice, washed
2 tablespoons olive oil
½ teaspoon Turkish
pepper flakes
½ teaspoon ground
black pepper
120g lamb mince (20% fat)
2 tablespoons tomato purée
2 tablespoons butter
400ml boiling water
sea salt

Serves 4–6 (makes 12–14)

1. Blanch the cabbage leaves in a saucepan of boiling water for 4–5 minutes until soft. Refresh in ice cold water and drain.

2. Put the onion, rice, oil, pepper flakes, black pepper, lamb and a good pinch of salt into a mixing bowl and mix well.

3. Wring any excess moisture out of the cabbage leaves and tear them into large strips. If the stalk is a bit hard, place it on a chopping board and gently press down with your thumb. This will flatten the stalk without ripping the leaf. Roll a small piece of filling up in the cabbage leaves – they should end up about 5cm long and 1cm wide. Set aside.

4. Mix the tomato purée and butter in a small saucepan with a good pinch of salt and black pepper. Place the *dolma* in two layers on top of each other in the pan. Pour over the boiling water; there should be just enough to cover the *dolma*. Bring to the boil over a medium heat. Cover, reduce the heat to low, and cook for 30–35 minutes, or until the rice is tender. Leave to cool. Serve at room temperature with a little of the buttery tomato sauce over the top.

Balik Kroket – Sardine Croquettes

Balik kroket are eaten as a starter in fish restaurants along the Mediterranean coast. The crispy croquettes make the perfect *meze* dish and are wonderful served with a glass of chilled *raki*. The traditional recipe uses *lor peyniri*, a soft, stringy cheese that keeps the croquettes really moist. I have used mozzarella for ease – it has the same texture, but is easier to source.

500g potatoes, peeled and roughly chopped
2 tablespoons olive oil
350g sardine fillets
120g grated mozzarella cheese
a handful of finely chopped flat-leaf parsley leaves
a handful of finely chopped dill
2½ teaspoons Turkish pepper flakes
2 teaspoons baking powder
1 teaspoon dried mint
grated zest of 1 lemon
1 egg
60g breadcrumbs
vegetable oil, for shallow frying
sea salt and freshly ground black pepper
lemon wedges, to serve

Serves 4 (makes 12–15)

1. Cook the potatoes in a large saucepan of boiling water over a medium heat for 8–10 minutes, or until soft. Drain and mash.

2. Meanwhile, heat the olive oil in a non-stick frying pan over a medium heat and gently fry the sardine fillets for 2–3 minutes on each side, or until just cooked through. Discard the skin and transfer the fish to a mixing bowl. Remove any bones you can see.

3. Add the mashed potato, mozzarella, parsley, dill, Turkish pepper flakes, baking powder, dried mint, lemon zest and egg. Season with a good pinch of salt and black pepper and mix everything together. Roll a walnut-sized piece of the mixture into a ball and roll in the breadcrumbs. Repeat with the remaining mixture.

4. Heat 1½–2cm of vegetable oil in a deep pan over a medium–high heat. Fry the croquettes in small batches for 30–45 seconds on each side, or until golden and crispy. Remove with a slotted spoon and drain on kitchen paper. Serve immediately with lemon wedges.

Chargrilled Squid with Smoked Aubergine

The food along the Mediterranean coast is fresh-tasting and light. Seafood is always the star of the show, and fresh parsley, mint and oregano are used in abundance. This squid salad captures all the flavours from this region of Turkey – wonderfully soft, smoked aubergines, charred baby squid and a showering of lemon juice and fresh herbs. I love the contrasting flavours of the rich aubergine base and the fresh seafood topping . . . heaven.

1 large aubergine
4 tablespoons olive oil
1 tablespoon tahini paste
½ teaspoon Turkish pepper flakes
¼ teaspoon ground cumin
juice of ¼ lemon
350g baby squid, cleaned
a handful of finely chopped flat-leaf parsley leaves
1 teaspoon sumac
sea salt and freshly ground black pepper

Serves 4

1. Prick the aubergine all over with a skewer. Place over a medium gas flame and cook for 3–4 minutes on each side, turning four times, or until tender. You should be able to poke a skewer into the charred skin and straight through the flesh when it is cooked. Leave to cool.

2. When cool to the touch, remove and discard the burnt skin. Cut off the top of the aubergine and finely chop the flesh. Place in a mixing bowl and add 2 tablespoons of the olive oil and the tahini, Turkish pepper flakes, cumin, lemon juice and a good pinch of salt and black pepper. Mix together well.

3. Heat a griddle pan over a high heat. Put the squid into a mixing bowl and add the remaining oil and a pinch of salt and black pepper. Toss together and char on the griddle for 30–60 seconds on each side until just cooked.

4. To serve, tip the aubergine onto a serving dish and top with the squid. Scatter over the parsley and sprinkle over the sumac. Serve immediately.

Smoked Aubergine Yogurt

My dear friend and Aegean chef extraordinaire, Gökçen, makes this simple *meze* dish for me every time I go to his house. He has lived on the Aegean coast for years and is considered a real authority on the food of the region. His smoked aubergine yogurt is clean-tasting and alluring. The smoky aubergines, creamy yogurt, lemon and garlic all work beautifully together, and the result is like a lighter version of baba ganoush, which is made in a similar style, but enriched with thick tahini.

2 aubergines
1 tablespoon extra virgin olive oil
200g Greek yogurt
1 garlic clove, crushed
juice of ½ lemon
sea salt

Serves 4

1. Prick the aubergines all over with a skewer. Carefully place over a medium gas flame and cook for 3–4 minutes on each side, turning four times, or until tender. You should be able to poke a skewer into the charred skin and straight through the flesh when it is cooked. Set aside to cool.

2. When cool to the touch, remove and discard the burnt skin. Cut off the tops of the aubergines and finely chop the flesh. Place in a mixing bowl and add the oil, yogurt, garlic, lemon juice and a generous pinch of salt. Mix everything together thoroughly and serve.

Kiz Güzeli – Beetroot Dip

This beetroot dip is another vibrant *meze* dish from Izmir on the Western coast of Turkey, where it would traditionally be served during the winter months as a *meze* before red meat. The earthy beetroots cook slowly in the oven, intensifying the flavour, and the roasted garlic adds an incredible background musk. If you can't get hold of fresh beetroots, use the pre-cooked variety and just roast the garlic beforehand to give the same flavour. Don't add the lemon juice until you have tasted the finished dip, as prepared beets are already sour with vinegar.

600g beetroots, washed
and trimmed
1 garlic bulb
2 tablespoons olive oil
180g Greek yogurt
juice of ½ lemon
a small handful of mint leaves
sea salt and freshly ground
black pepper

Serves 4

1. Preheat the oven to 180°C/gas mark 4. Put the beetroots into a mixing bowl and add the garlic and oil. Season with salt and black pepper and mix well. Place in a small roasting dish and cook for 1½–2 hours until tender. Remove from the oven and leave to cool.

2. When cool, skin the beetroots and transfer the flesh to a blender. Squeeze the garlic cloves into the blender. Pulse to a fine paste and tip into a mixing bowl. Add the yogurt and lemon juice. Mix well and check the seasoning. Tip into a serving bowl, scatter over the mint leaves and serve immediately.

Fava Bean Dip

As my wonderful niece Daisy said to me last time I was preparing this fava bean dip, 'it smells like a wet dog'. It does smell odd when you are boiling the beans, but freshen them up with herbs and lemon juice and they make a meltingly soft dip, with a light, earthy flavour. Fava beans are available throughout Turkey and they are used both fresh and dried for different recipes. The traditional version of Turkish fava is served differently, set in the fridge and cut into cubes – far too fussy for me. I prefer this non-traditional version, served as a thick dip with rivulets of peppery olive oil glimmering all over it.

360g dried fava beans
2 handfuls of finely
chopped dill
4 tablespoons extra virgin olive
oil, plus extra for drizzling
juice of 1½ lemons
sea salt and freshly ground
black pepper

Serves 4

1. Put the beans into a saucepan and pour over 1½ litres of cold water. Bring to the boil over a medium heat and remove any red husks that float to the surface. Cover, reduce the heat to low and cook for 30–35 minutes, or until the beans have broken up. Drain in a colander and return to the pan.

2. Add the dill, oil, lemon juice and a generous pinch of salt and black pepper. Mash everything together into a textured paste. Check the seasoning and scoop into a serving dish. Cover and leave to cool to room temperature. Serve with extra olive oil drizzled over the top.

Haydari – Lemon, Garlic and Herb Yogurt

Meyhane (tavern) culture in Turkey is the original drinking culture, where the men get together to drink wine or *raki*, eat and chat. Dinner at these taverns can go on late into the night and songs will be sung as the evening goes on. *Haydari* is one of the classic *meyhane* dishes, made from a strained yogurt that is flavoured with lemon juice, garlic and herbs. Traditionally, the yogurt is hung overnight in muslin, allowing the excess moisture to drip out, so that it gets really thick and creamy. I have to admit that I am never that organised, so I just buy a thick Greek yogurt instead.

375g Greek yogurt
55g feta cheese
a handful of finely chopped mint leaves
a handful of finely chopped dill
1 garlic clove, crushed
juice of ½ lemon
1 tablespoon olive oil
20g walnuts, finely chopped
sea salt and freshly ground black pepper

Serves 4

1. Scoop the yogurt into a mixing bowl and add the feta, herbs, garlic, lemon juice, oil and a good pinch of salt and black pepper. Mix everything together thoroughly and pour into a serving dish.

2. Top with the walnuts and serve immediately.

3

pide & köfte

Pide and *köfte* are classic Turkish street foods.

Pide are like boat-shaped pizzas that are covered in meat, cheese and butter, and served as an afternoon snack or light dinner, often with plates of parsley and lemon wedges. Traditional *pide* are very meat-heavy and the best version comes from Samsun on the Black Sea, where the locals love cooking with pastry and butter. Some of the most popular *pide* include *kiymali pide* (see page 64) a closed meat *pide* from the Black Sea, *Konya pide* (see page 71), which has large hand-cut chunks of lamb on top, and *Kayseri pide* (see page 67), which is topped with shaved beef pastrami and egg.

Pide are not usually prepared at home – instead, hungry Turks head to their local *pide* salon to feast on these crispy treats. Cooked in old wood-burning ovens, the chefs prepare the *pide* on long, oar-like paddles and then transfer them to the oven to cook. Once golden, they are removed and finished with melted butter. Over time, *pide* have evolved to incorporate lighter toppings, like smoked aubergine, spinach and olives.

Köfte are little round or oval-shaped meat patties made using finely minced lamb or beef. They are a very old dish, found in some of the first Persian and Ottoman recipes, and now different varieties exist all across Turkey, with most towns and cities having their own recipe.

Köfte vary in flavour, from plain meat seasoned with just a little salt, to heavily spiced with black pepper or Turkish pepper flakes. Some even include finely chopped onion and herbs. They are fried or grilled on the barbecue and served with a sauce or sometimes just a pinch of ground cumin for extra seasoning. *Köfte* are a national treasure and very easy to prepare at home. Using good-quality mince with at least 20 per cent fat will give you the best *köfte* – they should be soft, juicy and full of flavour.

These two dishes are Turkish takeout – fast food that can be eaten on the go. Whether you're driving through the stunning plains of Anatolia, relaxing on the beautiful Mediterranean coast or exploring Adana, you can stop anywhere and eat delicious *pide* or *köfte*. Here, I have picked out some of the classics so you can recreate these perfect pick-me-ups at home.

Pide Dough

Pide are really easy to make. You just need a simple, well-seasoned dough made from fine flour, yeast, salt and water. The dough is best used straight away as it has the perfect flavour and texture when fresh. If you don't want to use all of the *pide* dough at the same time, pop any remaining dough into a freezer bag and store in the freezer for up to 2 weeks. Just take the bag out and thaw overnight before using.

7g sachet fast-action dried yeast
1 teaspoon caster sugar
300g 00 grade durum wheat flour, plus extra for dusting
2 teaspoons salt
2 tablespoons olive oil, plus extra for greasing
100ml ice-cold water
topping of your choice (see recipes on pages 64–74)
butter, for brushing

Makes 8 *pide* shells

1. Put the yeast and sugar in a small bowl and add 2 tablespoons of lukewarm water. Stir and set aside for a few minutes until the mixture begins to froth.

2. Sift the flour into a mixing bowl. Make a well in the centre and add the salt. Pour in the olive oil and yeast mixture. Start to combine with your hands, while slowly pouring in the ice-cold water. Continue until all the water is incorporated and the dough starts to stick together. If needed, add a few extra tablespoons of water to help the dough fully combine. Tip the dough out onto a floured board and knead for 5–6 minutes until shiny and stretchy. Place into an oiled mixing bowl, cover with a clean tea towel and leave for 30 minutes to rise.

3. Preheat the oven to 220°C/gas mark 7 and line a baking sheet with baking paper.

4. Cut the dough into 8 equal pieces. Use your hands to form each piece into an oval shape. Dust both sides with flour and roll out into a large boat shape. The dough should be really thin – you should be able to just about see the board through the dough. Once you are there, prick the dough all over with a fork. Carefully place on the prepared baking sheet.

5. Arrange your chosen topping down the middle of each *pide*, leaving a 2cm gap around the edges. Fold the edges in on themselves, all around the *pide*, so that you have a folded 1cm border. Starting at one end and using your thumb and forefinger, squeeze the pastry border together so that it crimps and stands up a little. Do this all the way around and squeeze the two ends together. You should end up with a boat shape. Bake for 8–10 minutes, or until the two pointy edges have slightly curled up and the sides are golden.

6. Meanwhile, melt the butter in the microwave or a small pan. Brush the melted butter all over the cooked *pide*, slice and serve immediately.

Kıymalı Pide – Black Sea *Pide*

When we visit my partner's family in Samsun, one of the biggest cities in the Black Sea region, we make *kıymalı pide* (Black Sea *pide*) every Sunday. This is the classic Samsun *pide*. We fry small pieces of beef with onions and cumin, then take the meat to the baker down the road. He wraps the filling in a thin pastry and bakes it until crispy in his magnificent old oven, before brushing a thick coating of butter generously over the top. It's almost impossible to resist the temptation to eat them on the walk home.

½ quantity of *pide* dough (see page 63), cut into 4 equal pieces
4 tablespoons butter
1 tablespoon olive oil
1 onion, very finely chopped
300g lamb mince (20 per cent fat)
½ teaspoon Turkish pepper flakes
2 handfuls of finely chopped flat-leaf parsley leaves
sea salt and freshly ground black pepper

Makes 4 *pide*

1. Preheat the oven to 220°/gas mark 7 and line a baking sheet with baking paper.

2. Melt 2 tablespoons of the butter with the olive oil in a frying pan over a medium heat. Add the onion and cook, stirring occasionally, for 3–4 minutes until soft. Add the lamb and fry, stirring, for 3–4 minutes until just cooked through. Add the Turkish pepper flakes and a good pinch of salt and black pepper. Add the parsley and mix everything together well. Remove from the heat and leave to cool.

3. Use your hands to form each piece of dough into an oval shape. Dust both sides with flour and roll out into a large boat shape. The dough should be really thin – you should be able to just about see the board through the dough. Once you are there, prick the dough all over with a fork. Carefully place onto the prepared baking sheet.

4. Arrange the lamb mixture down the middle of each *pide*, leaving a 2.5cm gap all around. Fold the edges over the top of the filling. Starting at one end and using your thumb and forefinger, squeeze the two sides together tightly over the filling. Your *pide* should look like a very long, thin baguette. Bake for 8–10 minutes, or until the two pointy edges have slightly curled up and the sides are golden.

5. Meanwhile, melt the remaining butter. Brush the melted butter all over the cooked *pide*, slice and serve immediately.

Kayseri Pide – Pastrami and Egg Pide

One afternoon in Samsun, I stumbled across an old *pide* shop called Gözde Pide Salouu. It had a huge wood-burning oven and the two brothers manning it made the best *pide* I have ever eaten. Their *pide*-de-resistance was a *kayseri pide* – a pastrami and egg *pide* made with the smoky dried beef pastrami that is loved all over Turkey. This *pide* is all about simple ingredients cooked to perfection. The idea is to tear pieces off and dip them into the egg yolk. You can buy Turkish pastrami at a Turkish food shop. It looks and tastes like parma ham, which is a great alternative if you eat pork. In Turkey, this would be made with *kaşar* (see page 70), but Cheddar works just as well.

½ quantity of *Pide* Dough (see page 63), cut into 4 equal pieces
140g Turkish beef pastrami
200g grated Cheddar cheese
4 eggs
Turkish pepper flakes

Makes 4 *pide*

1. Preheat the oven to 220°C/gas mark 7 and line a baking sheet with baking paper.

2. Use your hands to form each piece of dough into an oval shape. Dust both sides with flour and roll out into a large boat shape. The dough should be really thin – you should be able to just about see the board through the dough. Once you are there, prick the dough all over with a fork. Carefully place on the prepared baking sheet.

3. Tear the pastrami into pieces and drape it down the middle of each piece of dough, leaving a 2cm gap all around. Scatter over the cheese. Fold the edges in on themselves all around the *pide*, so that you have a 1cm border. Starting at one end and using your thumb and forefinger, squeeze the pastry border together so that it crimps and stands up a little. Do this all the way around and squeeze the two ends together. You should end up with a boat shape. Bake for 7 minutes.

4. Carefully crack an egg in the middle of each *pide*. Return to the oven for 4–5 minutes until the egg is just set and the edges are golden. Season with Turkish pepper flakes and serve immediately.

Sujuk Pide

This is Turkish fast food at its best: a perfectly cooked, crispy *pide*, topped with thinly sliced *sujuk* and melted cheese. You can find this *pide* in towns and cities across the land and everyone loves it. Traditionally in Turkey they would use a hard cheese called *kaşar*, which has a strong flavour and a great melting quality. Cheddar works just as well and is easy to get hold of. If you can't find *sujuk* (see page 15), use a good-quality shop-bought pepperoni instead (if you eat pork).

½ quantity of *Pide* Dough
(see page 63), cut into
4 equal pieces
4 tablespoons tomato purée
100g *sujuk*, thinly sliced
300g grated Cheddar cheese
1 tablespoon butter

Makes 4 *pide*

1. Preheat the oven to 220°C/gas mark 7 and line a baking sheet with baking paper.

2. Use your hands to form each piece of *pide* dough into an oval shape. Dust both sides with flour and roll out into a large boat shape. The dough should be really thin – you should be able to just about see the board through the dough. Once you are there, prick the dough all over with a fork. Carefully place on the prepared baking sheet.

3. Spread the tomato purée down the middle of each *pide*, leaving a 2cm gap all around. Tear the *sujuk* into pieces and place it over the purée, followed by the cheese. Fold the edges in on themselves all around the *pide*, so that you have a 1cm border. Starting at one end, and using your thumb and forefinger, squeeze the pastry border together so that it crimps and stands up a little. Do this all the way around and squeeze the two ends together. You should end up with a boat shape. Bake for 10–12 minutes, or until the two pointy edges have slightly curled up and the sides are golden.

4. Meanwhile, melt the butter in the microwave or a small pan. Brush the melted butter all over the cooked *pide*, slice and serve immediately.

Konya *Pide*

Konya is a town in the middle of the central Anatolian region of Turkey. This beautiful city houses the stunning blue-tiled temple of Mevlana (see photo on page 164), home to the Persian mystic Rumi and the order of the Whirling Dervishes. The temple is truly beautiful, with towering minarets that stick out from a huge domed roof. Just as famous is the Konya *pide*, a very thin, crispy, boat-shaped pizza that is topped with lamb and lots of butter. It is served with mountains of fresh parsley and lemon wedges, and, to me, is as incredible as the temple.

½ quantity of *Pide* Dough
(see page 63), cut into
4 equal pieces
200g lamb mince
(20 per cent fat)
1 onion, very finely chopped
a handful of finely chopped
flat-leaf parsley leaves, plus
extra to serve
4 tablespoons tomato purée
2 tablespoons butter
sea salt and freshly ground
black pepper
lemon wedges, to serve

Makes 4 *pide*

1. Preheat the oven to 220°C/gas mark 7 and line a baking sheet with baking paper.

2. Use your hands to form each piece of dough into an oval shape Dust both sides with flour and roll out into a large boat shape. The dough should be really thin – you should be able to just about see the board through the dough. Once you are there, prick the dough all over with a fork. Carefully place on the prepared baking tray.

3. Put the lamb, onion and parsley into a mixing bowl, season with salt and black pepper, and mix well.

4. Spread the tomato purée down the middle of each *pide*, leaving a 2cm gap all around. Spread the meat mixture over the top in a thin layer. Fold the edges in on themselves all around the *pide*, so that you have a 1cm border. Starting at one end and using your thumb and forefinger, squeeze the pastry border together so that it crimps and stands up a little. Do this all the way around and squeeze the two ends together. You should end up with a boat shape. Bake for 10–12 minutes, or until the two pointy edges have slightly curled up and the sides are golden.

4. Meanwhile, melt the butter in a microwave or a small pan. Brush over the top of the cooked *pide* and serve immediately with lemon wedges and parsley.

Spinach *Pide*

Traditional *pide* are made with lots of meat and butter. Spinach *pide* is a modern version that is much lighter. The *pide* are flavoured with spinach, onions, cheese and a background hint of cumin. The trick here is making sure that the pan is really hot when you cook the spinach, so that it cooks quickly and doesn't go watery, meaning the *pide* stays perfectly crispy.

½ quantity *Pide* Dough
(see page 63), cut into
4 equal pieces
1 tablespoon olive oil
1 onion, finely chopped
200g baby spinach
½ teaspoon ground cumin
½ teaspoon freshly ground
black pepper
280g grated Cheddar cheese
sea salt

Makes 4 *pide*

1. Preheat the oven to 220°C/gas mark 7 and line a baking sheet with baking paper.

2. Use your hands to form each piece of dough into an oval shape. Dust both sides with flour and roll out into a large boat shape. The dough should be really thin – you should be able to just about see the board through the dough. Once you are there, prick the dough all over with a fork. Carefully place onto the prepared baking sheet.

3. Heat the oil in a frying pan over a high heat. Add the onion and fry for 3–4 minutes until golden. Add the spinach and fry for 2–3 minutes until wilted. Add the cumin, black pepper and a good pinch of salt. Mix well, remove from the heat and leave to cool for a few minutes.

4. Arrange the spinach down the middle of each *pide*, leaving a 2cm gap around the edges. Scatter over the cheese. Fold the edges in on themselves all around the *pide*, so that you have a 1cm border. Starting at one end and using your thumb and forefinger, squeeze the pastry border together so that it crimps and stands up a little. Do this all the way around and squeeze the two ends together. You should end up with a boat shape. Bake for 8–10 minutes, or until the two pointy edges have slightly curled up and the sides are golden. Serve immediately.

Chicken, Artichoke and Olive *Pide*

These *pide* make the perfect light lunch, served hot from the oven with a side salad. I have used olives and artichokes, classic flavours from the Mediterranean coast of Turkey, along with shredded chicken and cheese. In Turkey, cheese is very popular, and there is a huge variety of interesting local cheeses. Something like *kaşar*, a hardish yellow cheese, would be more traditionally used here, but Cheddar has a similar flavour and is easier to find outside Turkey.

½ quantity *Pide* Dough (see page 63), cut into 4 equal pieces
200g cooked chicken, shredded
200g griddled artichoke hearts in oil, drained
80g pitted black olives, roughly sliced
280g grated Cheddar cheese
sea salt and freshly ground black pepper

Makes 4 *pide*

1. Preheat the oven to 220°C/gas mark 7 and line a baking sheet with baking paper.

2. Use your hands to form each of the pieces of dough into an oval shape. Dust both sides with flour and roll out into a large boat shape. The dough should be really thin – you should be able to just about see the board through the dough. Once you are there, prick the dough all over with a fork. Carefully place onto the prepared baking sheet.

3. Arrange the chicken and artichokes down the middle of each *pide*, leaving a 2cm gap all around. Scatter over the olives and cheese. Fold the edges in on themselves all around the pide, so that you have a 1cm border. Starting at one end, and using your thumb and forefinger, squeeze the pastry border together so that it crimps and stands up a little. Do this all the way around and squeeze the two ends together. You should end up with a boat shape. Bake for 10–12 minutes, or until the two pointy edges have slightly curled up and the sides are golden. Serve immediately.

Aubergine and Lamb *Köfte*

Originally from Adana but hugely popular throughout Eastern Turkey, these incredible *köfte* are made with aubergines and lamb. The aubergines are smoked, finely chopped and mixed into softened tomatoes, spring onions and Turkish pepper. Lusciously spiced *köfte* are then fried until golden and served nestled into the aubergines. Often, this dish is served with *balon pide*, a very thin bread that puffs up like a balloon in the oven. It is perfect for scooping up the aubergine and rolling around the delicious lamb *köfte*.

2 aubergines
4 tablespoons olive oil
4 tomatoes, skinned and finely chopped
4 spring onions, finely sliced
4 Turkish green peppers, finely sliced
juice of ½ lemon
300g lamb mince
4 garlic cloves
1 slice of bread, crusts removed, soaked in 3 tablespoons water
1 teaspoon freshly ground black pepper
2 teaspoons ground cumin
1 teaspoon Turkish pepper flakes
a handful of finely chopped flat-leaf parsley leaves
sea salt
lemon wedges, to serve

Serves 4 (makes 12 *köfte*)

1. Prick the aubergines all over with a skewer. Carefully place them over a medium gas flame and cook for 3–4 minutes on each side, turning four times, or until tender. You should be able to poke a skewer into the charred skin and straight through the flesh when it is cooked. Leave to cool. When cool to the touch, remove and discard the burnt skin. Cut off the tops and finely chop the flesh.

2. Heat 2 tablespoons of the oil in a frying pan over a medium heat. Add the tomatoes, spring onions and green peppers. Mix well and cook, stirring occasionally, for 5–6 minutes until the tomatoes have just started to break down. Add the cooked aubergines and lemon juice, and season with salt. Mix together, remove from the heat and set aside.

3. Put the lamb in a large mixing bowl and crush over the garlic. Add the soaked bread, black pepper, cumin, Turkish pepper flakes and a good pinch of salt. Using your hands, mix together thoroughly for 5–6 minutes to help tenderise the meat. Take a walnut-sized piece of meat, roll it into a ball and flatten into an oval shape. Repeat with the rest of the meat.

4. Heat the remaining oil in a large frying pan over a medium heat. Fry the *köfte* for 2–3 minutes on each side until just cooked through. To serve, transfer the aubergines to a large serving dish and arrange the *köfte* over the top. Scatter over the parsley and serve with lemon wedges.

Sea Bass *Köfte* with Smoked Pepper Sauce

Levrek, or sea bass, is hugely popular in Turkey and enjoyed all along the Aegean and Mediterranean coastlines, where it is pan-fried, salt-baked or stewed. This simple *köfte* recipe is one of the few fish *köfte* found in Turkey, as they generally tend to be meat based. The sea bass can really take on the big flavours of the dried herbs and spices. I have also added bicarbonate of soda: you might associate this more with baking, but as any good Turkish cook will tell you, this secret ingredient keeps *köfte*, minced kebabs and fishcakes really light and fluffy.

2 red peppers, deseeded and cut into quarters
3 tablespoons olive oil
2 tablespoons Greek yogurt
juice of ½ lemon, plus a little extra for the peppers
350g sea bass fillets, skinned and boned
a handful of finely chopped flat-leaf parsley leaves
40g breadcrumbs
1 egg
1 teaspoon freshly ground black pepper
½ teaspoon dried thyme
½ teaspoon sumac
¼ teaspoon bicarbonate of soda
sea salt and freshly ground black pepper

Serves 4 (makes 8 *köfte*)

1. Preheat the oven to 200°C/gas mark 6.

2. Put the red peppers in a mixing bowl, add 1 tablespoon of the oil and season with salt and black pepper. Mix well and tip onto a baking tray. Roast for 30–35 minutes, or until the skin is charred and the peppers are tender. Tip the peppers into a mixing bowl, cover with cling film and leave for 10 minutes. When cooled, remove the skins and then whizz the flesh into a paste using a mini food processor. Pour the puréed pepper into a mixing bowl, add the yogurt and a tiny squeeze of lemon and mix well. Transfer to a small saucepan and keep warm over a low heat, stirring occasionally, until ready to use.

3. Meanwhile, put the fish into a food processor or blender and pulse until finely chopped. Tip into a mixing bowl and add the parsley, breadcrumbs, egg, black pepper, thyme, sumac, bicarbonate of soda and a pinch of salt. Mix well and divide into eight equal portions. Roll each one into a ball and then flatten into a round patty just under 1cm thick.

4. Heat the remaining oil in large pan over a medium heat. Fry the *köfte* for 2½–3 minutes on each side, until golden and cooked through. Squeeze over the lemon juice and serve immediately with the warm pepper sauce.

İçli Köfte – Stuffed Meatball *Köfte*

İçli köfte, or stuffed meatball *köfte*, are famous throughout Turkey. Originally from Gaziantep in East Turkey, these deep-fried lamb *köfte* are served as a *meze* dish before a kebab. A thick bulgur and lamb casing is stuffed with a lamb and nut filling, then rolled into cone shapes and deep fried. The outer casing goes gorgeously golden and crispy, and the inside stays juicy and rich. They taste incredible served hot with a dollop of creamy yogurt and a squeeze of lemon.

1 onion, roughly chopped
250g lamb mince
300g bulgur wheat
50g breadcrumbs
1 teaspoon Turkish pepper flakes
vegetable oil, for deep-frying
sea salt and freshly ground black pepper

For the filling
200g lamb mince
½ onion, finely chopped
10g walnuts, finely ground
10g pistachios, ground
10g ground almonds

Serves 4 (makes 8 *köfte*)

1. Put the onion in a food processor and blend until fine. Add the lamb mince, bulgur wheat, breadcrumbs and Turkish pepper flakes, season with salt and blend for 5 minutes, stopping regularly to scrape the sides so that the lamb gets really fine. Halfway through blending, add 5 tablespoons of cold water to help bind everything together.

2. Meanwhile, put all the filling ingredients into a mixing bowl and season with a generous pinch of salt and black pepper. Mix together thoroughly.

3. Take a golf ball-sized piece of the first mixture and, on a clean surface, roll it out into a circle about the size of a small fried egg. Place a walnut-sized piece of the filling in the middle. Pull one half of the outer layer over into a half-moon shape. Wet your hands with a little water and roll the *köfte* into a tight cone shape. Repeat with the remaining ingredients to make 8 *köfte*.

4. Heat the oil in a large frying pan over a medium heat. Drop a small piece of the outer layer into the oil. It will sink. When it bubbles up to the surface the oil is hot enough. Fry the *köfte*, two or three at a time, for 8–10 minutes until golden and cooked through. Drain on kitchen paper. Repeat with the rest and serve immediately

Hasan Pasha Köfte – Cheesy Beef *Köfte*

These *Hasan Pasha köfte* are named after Hasan Pasha, the Ottoman ruler of Algiers in the 15th century. They were presented to him at an epic dinner at the Sultan's palace after he won many great victories for the empire. The *köfte* are like a miniature meal in themselves – little beef *köfte* are topped with mashed potato and *lor peyniri*, a soft, stringy, mozzarella-like cheese, then baked in a tomato sauce. To make sure that your *köfte* stay moist, keep them snug in a small baking dish and, if you think they are looking too dry, add an extra splash of water. *Lor peyniri* is hard to come by outside of Turkey, so use a good-quality mozzarella instead.

300g potatoes, peeled and cut into chunks
1 tablespoon butter
1 egg, separated
½ teaspoon Turkish pepper flakes
500g beef mince (15 per cent fat minimum)
½ onion, finely chopped
1 garlic clove, crushed
1 teaspoon freshly ground black pepper
1 slice of bread, crusts removed, soaked in 3 tablespoons cold water
125ml tomato passata
75g grated mozzarella cheese
a small handful of torn flat-leaf parsley leaves
sea salt

Serves 4 (makes 8 *köfte*)

1. Preheat the oven to 200°C/gas mark 6.

2. Cook the potatoes in a pan of boiling water until tender, drain and return to the pan. Add the butter, egg yolk, Turkish pepper flakes and a good pinch of salt. Mash together until smooth and set aside.

3. Meanwhile, put the beef mince in a mixing bowl and add the onion, garlic, black pepper, soaked bread, egg white and a good pinch of salt. Using your hands, mix together thoroughly for a few minutes. The mixture will feel wet at first, but the bread will begin to absorb the moisture. Roll into eight meatballs and place them in a snug ovenproof dish. Push your thumb into the centre of each meatball and create a well. Top each *köfte* with a spoonful of the cooked potatoes.

4. Mix the passata with 125ml cold water and pour around the *köfte*. Cover the dish with foil and cook for 15–20 minutes, or until just cooked through. Scatter over the cheese and return to the oven for 2–3 minutes until melted. Sprinkle with parsley and serve.

Akçaabat Beef *Köfte*

A few years ago, we were driving along the coast of the windswept Black Sea towards the Georgian border and had stopped at a tiny café near the town of Akçaabat. This 'café' was, more accurately, a huge kettle slung over an open fire, with a little grill for *köfte* and few tables huddled together. We sipped tea and admired the view, watching the fishermen cast their nets into the silvery-grey waters of the Black Sea. Then came huge plates of *köfte*, chopped salad and freshly baked bread. The *köfte* were beef and spiked with lots of black pepper and parsley. They warmed us up beautifully. I hope you enjoy them as much as we did.

350g beef mince
1 onion, finely chopped
a handful of finely chopped flat-leaf parsley leaves
2 teaspoons freshly ground black pepper
1 teaspoon Turkish pepper flakes
½ teaspoon ground cumin
25g dried breadcrumbs
1 egg
¼ teaspoon bicarbonate of soda
vegetable oil, for frying
sea salt

Serves 4 (makes 12 *köfte*)

1. Put all the ingredients, minus the oil, in a mixing bowl. Add a large pinch of salt and, using your hands, mix the ingredients together for 5–6 minutes to tenderise the meat.

2. Take a walnut-sized piece of the mixture, roll it into a ball and flatten it into a 2.5mm thick, oval shaped *köfte*. Repeat with the remaining mixture. Place the *köfte* on a tray and refrigerate for 20 minutes.

3. Brush a griddle pan with a little oil and heat over a high heat until smoking. Reduce the heat to medium and cook the *köfte* for 3–4 minutes on each side, or until golden and cooked through. Serve immediately.

4

kebabs

Smoky, charred, juicy and delicious,

Turkish kebabs are the best in the world. Over the centuries, the Turkish people have perfected the best techniques for grilling meat and turned it into an art form. Now let me be very clear, true Turkish kebabs are vastly different to the distant cousin you may have eaten late at night on the way home from the pub. Traditional Turkish kebabs are a thing of beauty. From grilled kebabs on long metal skewers to döner kebabs turning slowly on the heat, or Iskender kebabs that are sliced onto bread and covered in sauce, there are many varieties to choose from, each more delicious than the last.

Kebabs are an old food, eaten across Persia and Constantinople for centuries. The origins can be found in the Persian word *kebab*, which was given to the meat that soldiers skewered onto their swords and cooked over hot coals. Now, *mangal* (barbecue) restaurants across Turkey serve grilled kebabs to hungry diners for a quick lunch or long dinner. Huge indoor barbecue pits with massive extractors are the centrepiece and skewered kebabs are expertly cooked over the hot coals and served with bread, salads and meze.

For the perfect kebab, the meat should come from a young male lamb, ideally 9 months old. For minced meat kebab, a mix of leg, shoulder and belly, with at least 40 per cent fat, is meticulously hand chopped until fine using a mighty meat cleaver called a *zırh*. The curved blade looks like a huge mezzaluna with one handle – it is the perfect shape to roll over the meat and cut it to the right consistency really quickly.

While you can ask your butcher to do this for you, I find using a good shop-bought mince with 20 per cent fat that is given a good blast in the blender will give you a lovely juicy kebab at home. I have recipes for some of the most classic kebabs in Turkey, from the spicy Adana kebab (see page 90) to the fragrant Iskender kebab (see page 95), each adapted so that you can make them at home without the need for an indoor barbecue.

Spicy Adana Kebabs

This is one of my favourite kebabs and I think I'm safe in saying that that is true for most of Turkey, too. Named after the city of Adana in the south east, this kebab is very simple – and very spicy. Fatty lamb is hand-chopped with salt and masses of Turkish pepper flakes, which give the dish its distinctive hot flavour and slight reddish colour. The lamb is fed onto flat metal skewers and cooked over hot coals. It is served on a flatbread with parsley, green peppers and tomatoes on the side.

½ onion, roughly chopped
½ red pepper, deseeded and roughly chopped
450g lamb mince (20 per cent fat)
2 teaspoons Turkish pepper flakes
2 tablespoons olive oil
sea salt

Serves 4 (makes 4 kebabs)

1. Put the onion and red pepper into a food processor or blender and give them a good blitz until fine. Add the lamb, Turkish pepper flakes and a good pinch of salt, and blend for 2–3 minutes until really fine. Tip the mixture into a mixing bowl, cover and refrigerate for 30 minutes.

2. Preheat the grill or barbecue to high. Divide the mixture into four equal portions and roll each one into a sausage shape. Flatten slightly and thread on to a skewer. Rub all over with oil. Place on the hot griddle and cook for 3–4 minutes on each side or until charred on the outside and just cooked through in the middle. Serve immediately.

Ali Nazik – Minced Lamb and Smoked Aubergine

Ali nazik originated in the Eastern town of Gazientep, which has some of the best food in Turkey. The dish was prepared for a sultan in the 16th century and he asked whose 'gentle hand', or 'eli nazik' had made it – and so the dish was born. Traditionally in Turkish, the word 'kebab' means anything that is cooked over charcoal; something that Turkish culture excels in. This particular kebab would involve cooking the mince in a pan over hot coals to take on the smoky hues. You can try this at home on your barbecue, otherwise it works just as well on the hob.

2 aubergines
200g Greek yogurt
2 tablespoons olive oil
500g lamb mince
(20 per cent fat)
2 teaspoons tomato purée
2½ teaspoons Turkish
pepper flakes
½ teaspoon dried oregano
30g butter
a handful of chopped
flat-leaf parsley leaves
sea salt and freshly ground
black pepper
flatbreads, to serve

Serves 4

1. Prick the aubergines all over with a skewer. Carefully place over a medium gas flame and cook for 3–4 minutes on each side, turning four times, or until tender. You should be able to poke a skewer into the charred skin and straight through the flesh when it is cooked. Leave to cool. When cool to the touch, remove and discard the burnt skin. Cut off the tops and finely chop the flesh. Tip into a mixing bowl and add the yogurt and a generous pinch of salt and black pepper. Mix together really well.

2. Meanwhile, heat the oil in a frying pan over a high heat and add the lamb. Fry for 8–10 minutes until golden. Add the tomato purée, 1 teaspoon of the Turkish pepper flakes, the oregano and a good pinch of salt. Mix together and then remove from the heat.

3. Put the butter in a small pan and heat for 1–2 minutes over a medium heat until bubbling. Add the remaining Turkish pepper flakes and mix well. Remove from the heat and leave for a few minutes to infuse.

4. To serve, spread the glorious aubergines out onto a serving platter. Spoon over the golden nuggets of lamb and scatter over the parsley. Drizzle over the red butter and serve immediately with warm flatbreads.

My Iskender Kebab

Iskender is one of the most popular Turkish kebabs. It was invented in the city of Bursa in the north west of Turkey. In 1850, a restaurant owner called Iskender decided to cook spit-roast lamb vertically, and so invented the *döner* kebab. Not content with just this, he served his sliced *döner* on freshly baked flatbread and covered it with a rich tomato sauce and thick yogurt. The Iskender kebab was born and it is now eaten all over Turkey. The likelihood is that you won't have the tools to make your own *döner* at home, so I have created a twist on the original, using charred steaks so that it is a bit easer.

3 white tortilla wraps
2 rib-eye steaks (about 250g each)
1 tablespoon olive oil
30g butter
2 tablespoons tomato purée
½ teaspoon Turkish pepper flakes
130g Greek yogurt
1 garlic clove, crushed
juice of ½ lemon
sea salt and freshly ground black pepper

Serves 4

1. Roll the wraps up and cut them with a pair of scissors over a serving dish into 0.5cm strips.

2. Heat a griddle pan over a high heat. Season the steaks with salt and black pepper and rub each one with a little oil. Cook for 2½–3 minutes each side until rare. Place the cooked steaks on top of the shredded wraps and cover with clingfilm for 5 minutes to rest.

3. Meanwhile, put the butter, tomato purée, Turkish pepper flakes and a pinch of salt into a pan and mix well. Heat over a medium heat for 1–2 minutes until melted.

4. Put the yogurt, garlic, lemon juice and a pinch of salt into a mixing bowl and mix together.

5. Slice up the steak and return it to the wraps. Dollop over the yogurt and drizzle the hot tomato sauce over everything. Serve immediately.

Kilis Kebab – Lamb Meatball Kebab

My first experience of this delicious dish was in east Turkey, when I was at lunch with the mayor of Gaziantep (as you do). The chef wanted to make something special so he served *Kilis* kebab, named after the town of Kilis, known for its rich kebab culture. Lamb meatballs and aubergine chunks are skewered together and cooked over charcoal until smoky. They are then de-skewered and transferred into a rich tomato sauce to finish cooking. The end result is sublime. Although I have pan-fried the meatballs and aubergines for my *Kilis* kebab, feel free to go all the way and cook them on a barbecue to get a more authentic flavour.

4 tablespoons olive oil
2 Turkish green peppers, finely sliced
2 onions, finely chopped
2 garlic cloves, finely sliced
2 tablespoons red pepper paste
2 tablespoons tomato purée
juice of ½ lemon
1 teaspoon freshly ground black pepper
400g tin chopped tomatoes
1 aubergine, half the skin removed in strips
350g lamb mince (20 per cent fat)
1 tablespoon vegetable oil
sea salt

Serves 4

1. Heat the olive oil in a large frying pan over a medium heat. Add the peppers and onions and mix well. Cook, stirring occasionally, for 8–10 minutes until really golden and soft. Add the garlic, mix well and cook for 10 seconds until fragrant. Add the red pepper paste, tomato purée, lemon juice, black pepper, tomatoes and a good pinch of salt. Pour in 200ml of cold water and mix together. Bring to the boil, cover, reduce the heat to low and cook gently for 1 hour.

2. Meanwhile, cut the half-peeled aubergine into quarters lengthways. Cut each quarter into three large pieces.

3. Put the lamb into a mixing bowl and season with a good pinch of salt. Mix together really well. Take a walnut-sized piece of mince and roll it into a ball. Repeat with the rest.

4. Heat the vegetable oil in a non-stick pan over a high heat until smoking. Add the meatballs and cook for 2 minutes on the top and bottom, until golden all over. Remove from the pan and set aside. Add the aubergine pieces and cook for 2–3 minutes on just one side until really smoky and charred. Remove from the pan and leave to cool. Once cool, cut any larger pieces of aubergine in half, so that they are about 2–2.5cm. If you cut them this small before charring, they would lose their texture.

5. Add the aubergine pieces to the sauce, cover and cook for 30 minutes. Gently mix together and then add the meatballs. Shake the pan so that they settle into the sauce and then cover and cook for 25–30 minutes, or until the meatballs are just cooked through and the sauce wonderfully rich. Serve immediately.

Lamb Kebabs in a Smoky Tomato Sauce

This is a great dish to serve when you have friends over for dinner: juicy lamb kebabs sitting on top of a rich tomato sauce. All you need then is a big salad and lots of bread, and everyone will be very happy. This recipe was inspired by a Turkish *kıyma kebabı*, a classic minced meat kebab that is similar to the Adana kebab (see page 90), but has a milder flavour. It is hugely popular in the eastern towns of Adana, Gaziantep, Urfa and Mersin, which have all soaked up the kebab culture from Persia centuries before.

2 tomatoes, halved
1 onion, quartered
1 Turkish green pepper, roughly sliced
1½ tablespoons tomato purée
½ teaspoon caster sugar
sea salt and freshly ground black pepper

For the kebab
½ red pepper, deseeded and roughly chopped
a handful of flat-leaf parsley leaves
1 garlic clove
450g lamb mince (20 per cent fat)
1 teaspoon freshly ground black pepper
1 teaspoon Turkish pepper flakes
2 tablespoon vegetable oil

Serves 4 (makes 4 kebabs)

1. Heat a griddle pan over a high heat until smoking. Put the tomatoes on the hot griddle, flesh-side down, and scatter the onion and green pepper around them. Cook for 4–5 minutes until charred. Remove from the pan and put in a food processor or blender. Add the tomato purée, sugar, 150ml of cold water and a good pinch of salt and black pepper. Blend until completely smooth. Pour into a small saucepan, cover and cook over a low heat, stirring occasionally, for 1 hour, or until the sauce has reduced by half and is really thick.

2. Meanwhile, prepare the kebab. Put the red pepper, parsley and garlic into a food processor or blender and blitz until fine. Add the lamb, black pepper, Turkish pepper flakes and a good pinch of salt. Blend for 3–4 minutes, until the meat sticks together like dough. Place into an oiled mixing bowl, cover and refrigerate for 30 minutes or up to 2 hours.

3. Heat a griddle pan over a high heat. Divide the meat mixture into four equal portions and roll each one into a 10cm sausage shape. Gently flatten using two fingers all the way along, so each sausage is about 2.5cm wide. Brush both sides of each kebab with a little vegetable oil. Carefully place on the griddle and cook for 2 ½–3 minutes on each side, until charred and just cooked through.

4. To serve, pour the hot sauce onto a serving dish and place the just-cooked kebabs on top. Leave to rest for 1 minute before serving.

Simit Kebab with Lamb and Pistachios

This special kebab gets its name from the Arabic word 'semiz', which means semolina or hard wheat. And it is the hard bulgur wheat that is mixed with the ground lamb that gives the *simit* kebab its nutty flavour and wonderful texture. I love to dress up these kebabs with a drizzle of yogurt and a sprinkling of bright green pistachio nuts.

35g shelled pistachios
a handful of flat-leaf parsley leaves
a handful of mint leaves
½ onion, roughly chopped
2 garlic cloves
450g lamb mince (20 per cent fat)
1 teaspoon Turkish pepper flakes
25g bulgur, soaked in the same volume of boiling water for 10 minutes, then drained
2 tablespoons vegetable oil
sea salt and freshly ground black pepper
yogurt and ground pistachios, to serve

Serves 4 (makes 4 kebabs)

1. Put the pistachios into a food processor or blender and blend until fine. Add the herbs and give them a blitz until they are finely chopped. Add the onion and garlic and blend until fine. Add the lamb, Turkish pepper flakes, bulgur and a generous pinch of salt and black pepper. Mix together for 4–5 minutes or until the meat sticks together like dough. You will need to stop and scrape down the sides every now and then. Tip the blended mixture into an oiled mixing bowl. Cover and refrigerate for 30 minutes or up to 2 hours.

2. Heat a griddle pan over a high heat until smoking. Divide the meat mixture into four equal pieces and roll each one into a 10cm sausage shape. Brush with a little vegetable oil. Cook for 8–10 minutes, turning every 2–2 ½ minutes until cooked through and juicy. Serve immediately with a drizzle of yogurt and the ground pistachios over the top.

Gaziantep Lamb Cutlets

This recipe is based on a very simple lamb kebab that I first tasted in Gaziantep. Traditionally it would be made using chunks of lamb, marinated until terrifically tender, then cooked furiously over hot coals. I have slightly adapted the recipe to use lamb cutlets instead. Like the original, the lamb is tenderised overnight in a thick, spicy marinade and then cooked until charred. I have used a griddle pan for this recipe, but feel free to cook the cutlets on the barbecue for a more sophisticated smoky finish.

750g lamb rack cutlets
3 tablespoons Greek yogurt
2 tablespoons olive oil
1 teaspoon Turkish
pepper flakes
1 teaspoon dried mint
2 garlic cloves, crushed
2 teaspoons tomato purée
1 ripe tomato, skinned and
deseeded
sea salt

Serves 4

1. Put the lamb cutlets into a mixing bowl and season with a good pinch of salt. Add the yogurt, 1 teaspoon of the oil, the Turkish pepper flakes, mint, garlic and tomato purée. Squish the tomato between your hands and let it ooze through your hands into the mix: the tomato will help tenderise the meat and keep it moist. Mix everything together thoroughly so that all the lamb gets coated. Cover and marinate overnight in the fridge.

2. When ready to cook, remove the lamb cutlets from the fridge and allow them to come to room temperature. Preheat the grill to high. Drizzle the remaining oil over the cutlets and grill them for 6–8 minutes each side, until golden on the outside and pink in the middle. Serve immediately.

Tepsi Kebab – Tray Kebab

Turkish people love to eat and as a result most of them are good home cooks. However, they still like to eat out, and kebab is one of the most popular dishes to go out for. It makes sense, as making perfect kebabs usually requires a huge grill with masses of charcoal and space. However, this east Turkish *tepsi kebab* is cooked in the oven, so it's easy to make at home. A lamb stew, flavoured with black pepper, thyme, oregano and cumin, is poured over aubergines that have been cooked in hot oil. This is finished in the oven, so that the aubergines absorb all the flavours of the lamb stew.

vegetable oil, for shallow frying
2 aubergines, half the skin removed in strips, then cut into 5mm thick rounds
1½ tablespoons olive oil
1 tablespoon butter
2 onions, finely chopped
500g leg of lamb, cut into bite-sized pieces
1 tablespoon red pepper paste
1 teaspoon freshly ground black pepper
1 teaspoon dried thyme
1 teaspoon dried oregano
1 bay leaf
1 teaspoon ground cumin
1 teaspoon Turkish pepper flakes
400g tin chopped tomatoes
sea salt

Serves 4

1. Heat 5mm vegetable oil in a frying pan over a medium heat and fry the aubergines, in two batches, for 6–8 minutes until golden. Remove from the pan and drain on kitchen paper.

2. Heat the olive oil and butter in a casserole dish over a medium heat and add the onions. Cook, stirring occasionally, for 5–6 minutes until translucent. Add the lamb, red pepper paste, black pepper, thyme, oregano, bay leaf, cumin, Turkish pepper flakes, tomatoes and a generous pinch of salt. Mix everything together really well. Cover, reduce the heat to low and cook for 1–1½ hours until tender. Remove the lid and turn the heat up to medium. Cook, stirring occasionally, for 15 minutes to thicken up. Check the seasoning.

3. Preheat the oven to 200°C/gas mark 6. Layer the fried aubergines in an ovenproof dish and spoon over the lamb and all the wonderful juices. Cover with foil and bake for 10 minutes to allow the flavours to mingle. Serve immediately.

Kürdan Kebabs

Kürdan means toothpick, and this is a toothpick kebab. Not that you need a toothpick after you've eaten it, more that you need one (or a cocktail stick) to help wrap soft slices of cooked aubergine around the peppery meatballs, keeping them wonderfully moist in the oven. Traditionally, this was served during Ramadan; now it tends to be cooked as a weeknight staple all over Turkey.

2 aubergines, cut lengthways into 6mm strips (you will need 16 slices)
olive oil, for frying
350g lamb mince (20 per cent fat)
½ onion, finely chopped
2 garlic cloves, crushed
1 teaspoon dried oregano
½ teaspoon ground cumin
½ teaspoon freshly ground black pepper
1 egg white
30g breadcrumbs
2 tablespoons olive oil
200ml tomato passata
sea salt

Serves 4 (makes 8 kebabs)

1. Heat a griddle pan over a high heat. Brush the aubergine slices with oil and griddle for 1–1½ minutes on each side until tender and charred. Set aside and leave to cool.

2. Put the lamb in a mixing bowl and add the onion, garlic, oregano, cumin, black pepper, egg white, breadcrumbs and a good pinch of salt. Mix together thoroughly and roll into eight balls. Heat the oil in a pan over a medium heat and cook the meatballs for 2 minutes, top and bottom, until golden all over.

3. Preheat the oven to 200°C/gas mark 6. Lay 2 aubergine strips on top of each other to make a cross. Place a meatball in the centre and fold up the strips around it. Fasten with a cocktail stick and put into a small ovenproof dish. Repeat with the remaining meatballs and aubergine slices. Pour over the passata and 150ml of cold water, cover with foil and bake for 20 minutes. Remove the foil and return to the oven for a further 5 minutes. Serve immediately.

Pomegranate Beef Skewers

The inspiration for these beef skewers came from a Turkish kebab called *çöp şiş*, an odds-and-ends sort of kebab, where leftover bits of meat are chopped up and marinated in yogurt and spices and then grilled. I first ate these at a smoky street stall on a warm evening in the town of Adana and quickly fell in love. The marinade tenderises the meat beautifully and the Turkish pepper flakes give it a little kick. For my kebab, I have been a bit more fancy and used a good piece of steak, marinated in the traditional way, and finished off with pomegranate molasses and honey: two flavours that work beautifully with the cooked beef.

600g rump steak, trimmed and cut into 3cm cubes
4½ tablespoons Greek yogurt
½ teaspoon Turkish pepper flakes
juice of 1 lemon
1 tablespoon olive oil
2 tablespoons pomegranate molasses
1 ½ teaspoons runny honey
sea salt and freshly ground black pepper

Serves 4 (makes 8–10 kebabs)

1. Put the beef in a mixing bowl and add the yogurt, Turkish pepper flakes and lemon juice. Season with salt and black pepper and mix well. Cover and marinate for 30 minutes or in the fridge overnight.

2. Preheat the grill or barbecue to high. Thread the meat onto wooden skewers. Brush with the oil and cook for 4–5 minutes on each side or until charred and tender.

3. Meanwhile, mix the pomegranate molasses and honey with 1 tablespoon of cold water and a pinch of salt in a mixing bowl. Drizzle over the cooked beef skewers and serve immediately.

Şiş Tavuk – Chicken Shish

Şiş tavuk is a classic Turkish kebab that is also found all over the Middle East, with its roots in Syria and the Persian Empire. It is also one of the simplest kebabs in terms of ingredients, but getting it right is an art form: the meat has to be very tender and juicy, perfectly charred and well seasoned. A great trick they use in Turkey is to squeeze half a tomato into the marinade – the acidity helps tenderise the meat and the sugars keep it sweet and help it turn a glorious golden colour as it cooks.

600g chicken thighs, cut into bite-sized pieces
4 tablespoons Greek yogurt
3 garlic cloves, crushed
1½ teaspoons freshly ground black pepper
2 teaspoons dried oregano
½ ripe tomato
2 tablespoons olive oil, plus extra for drizzling
sea salt
lemon wedges, to serve

Serve 4 (makes 8 kebabs)

1. Put the chicken pieces into a mixing bowl. Add the yogurt, garlic, black pepper, oregano and a good pinch of salt. Using your hands, squish the tomato into the bowl so that it breaks up. Mix it in well. Cover and marinate in the fridge for 2 hours or overnight.

2. Preheat the grill or barbecue to high. Meanwhile, thread the chicken onto skewers and rub a little oil all over them. Cook for 4–5 minutes on each side or until charred and cooked through. Serve immediately with lemon wedges.

Monkfish Kebabs

Although monkfish is found in the warm Mediterranean waters off the south coast of Turkey, it is not a hugely popular fish compared to *levrek* (sea bass) or *lüfer* (bluefish). But what I love about monkfish is that its big taste and firm texture can stand up to really robust flavours. It works beautifully cooked over a high heat, so it's perfect for kebabs. With simple Aegean ingredients, this recipe really captures the mood of the lighter cooking on the western coast of Turkey.

450g monkfish, cut into
2.5cm cubes
1 lemon, quartered
and then sliced
½ onion, quartered
2 garlic cloves, crushed
4 bay leaves, torn
¼ teaspoon Turkish
pepper flakes
2 tablespoons olive oil
sea salt and freshly ground
black pepper

Serves 4

1. Heat the griddle pan over a high heat. Mix all the ingredients together in a mixing bowl with a good pinch of salt and black pepper.

2. Thread the fish onto wooden skewers with a mixture of onion, lemon or bay leaf in between. Cook for 2–3 minutes on each side until just cooked through. Serve immediately.

Vegetable Kebabs

'Vegetable' and 'kebab' are not words that have much synergy together in Turkey. Kebabs are meat, end of story. However, while grilling up a batch of Chicken Shish (see page 108), vegetables are often skewered in between the meat to be eaten with flatbreads. Juicy tomatoes, bright green peppers and sweet onions char up beautifully, and the flavours really intensify. I love them with or without meat, so this is for all the vegetarians out there (and even if you're not, try this anyway).

4 red onions, halved

4 tomatoes

4 Turkish green peppers, halved

2 tablespoons olive oil

2 tablespoons pomegranate molasses

½ teaspoon Turkish pepper flakes

1 teaspoon dried oregano

a handful of mint leaves

sea salt and freshly ground black pepper

Serves 4 (makes 4 kebabs)

1. Heat a grill or barbecue to high. Put the onions, tomatoes and peppers in a mixing bowl, add the oil and season with salt and pepper. Mix well.

2. Thread the onions, tomatoes and peppers onto four skewers and cook for 4–5 minutes on each side until charred on the outside and tender on the inside.

3. Transfer to a serving dish and drizzle over the pomegranate molasses. Sprinkle over the Turkish pepper flakes, oregano and mint. Serve immediately.

chapter

5
salads

Turkish salads are simple, made with the best ingredients

and dressed in lemon juice and tangy pomegranate molasses. These sumptuous salads are served with every meal and the standard plate of parsley leaves comes with breakfast, lunch and dinner.

Traditional *meze*-style salads are still served in restaurants or at home before a big dinner. These include the classic aubergine salad made with chopped tomatoes and sweet onions; Haricot, Egg, Spring Onion and Tahini Salad (see page 124); Fried Halloumi (see page 131); and the simple 'Spoon Salad' (see page 116), a finely chopped, tangy treat.

In addition to these traditional dishes, there are fabulous modern salads that make the most of tantalising Turkish ingredients: fresh, fragrant herbs, juicy tomatoes, olives, sweet onions, seasonal vegetables and nutty wholegrains. Generous amounts of olive oil and lemon juice are used to make a basic dressing, and thick yogurt can be added for a creamier finish, giving everything a wonderfully tart, cooling flavour.

For something more substantial, try my Herby Chicken and Pearl Barley Salad (see page 132), made from a rustic mix of shredded cabbage, carrot and onion, traditionally served with a kebab dish. Or, to sample the lively flavours of the Aegean coast, try my Baby Octopus Salad (see page 136), bursting with tomatoes, fresh oregano, olives and lemon.

Classic Spoon Salad

This simple salad is served with most restaurant meals, with soft white bread to soak up all the tangy juices. It gets the name 'spoon salad' because all the ingredients have to be finely chopped so that they fit onto a small spoon. It is colourful, juicy and delicious. Once you have prepared it, leave the salad in the fridge for about half an hour to allow the flavours to intensify.

1 red onion, finely chopped
150g cherry tomatoes, quartered
¼ cucumber, deseeded and finely chopped
1 red pepper, deseeded and finely chopped
2 handfuls of finely chopped flat-leaf parsley leaves
1 handful of finely chopped mint leaves
juice of ½ lemon
2 tablespoons pomegranate molasses
1 tablespoon olive oil
40g walnuts, lightly crushed
sea salt and freshly ground black pepper

Serves 4

1. Put everything except the walnuts into a large mixing bowl and mix together thoroughly, seasoning to taste as you go.

2. Cover and leave for 20–30 minutes in the fridge for the flavours to develop. Tip onto a serving dish, top with the walnuts and serve immediately.

Olive and Herb Salad

Olive and herb salads are often served in the eastern regions of Turkey, as sides to a kebab. The tartness cuts through the richness of the fatty meat and seems to bring out the flavours of the kebab even more. Kebab or no kebab, this olive salad is fabulous. Crunchy, savoury and simple to make – what could be better?

55g walnuts, lightly crushed

250g pitted green olives, roughly sliced

1 red onion, finely chopped

2 handfuls of roughly chopped flat-leaf parsley leaves

2 handfuls of roughly chopped mint leaves

1 teaspoon Turkish pepper flakes

2 tablespoons olive oil

3 tablespoons pomegranate molasses

sea salt

Serves 4

1. Put all the ingredients into a large mixing bowl and add a small pinch of salt.

2. Toss together and tip onto a serving dish. Serve immediately.

Orange and Celeriac Salad

This salad is my version of a wonderfully unusual Ottoman dish called *portakalli zeytinyağli kereviz*, where celeriac is slowly braised with carrots, apple, orange and olive oil – all classic Aegean ingredients. Once cooked, it is left to cool and served at room temperature. It is quite incredible, with a floral smell and delicate flavour, and it is often served with eggs for a winter breakfast. I have taken the main ingredients of that dish and turned it into this zingy salad. Nutty, shaved celeriac provides the base, topped with sliced apple and chopped red onion and a light, citrusy dressing. It is fantastic with kebabs or plain grilled fish.

1 orange
250g celeriac, sliced with a mandolin
100g green apple, sliced with a mandolin
1 red onion, finely chopped
juice of ½ lemon
¼ teaspoon sumac
2 tablespoons olive oil
sea salt

Serves 4

1. Carefully peel the orange using a sharp knife. Cut out the segments and put them into a mixing bowl. Squeeze the juice of the remaining orange bits over the top.

2. Add the celeriac, apple, onion, lemon juice, sumac, olive oil and a good pinch of salt. Toss together and serve immediately.

Courgettes, Feta, Dill and Walnuts

Cevizli kabak is one of the staple cold salads that are served across Turkey. Instead of finely chopping everything and mixing it with yogurt in the traditional style, I have created a modern version, with griddled courgettes laid out on a platter and topped with a mix of feta, walnuts and griddled chilli strips, with yogurt drizzled over the top.

300g baby courgettes, finely sliced lengthways into thin strips
2 red chillies
2 tablespoons olive oil
50g Greek yogurt
1 garlic clove, crushed
juice of 1 lemon
20g walnuts, lightly crushed
55g feta cheese
a handful of finely chopped dill
sea salt and freshly ground black pepper

Serves 4

1. Heat a griddle pan over a high heat. Put the courgettes and chillies into a mixing bowl and add the olive oil. Season with salt and black pepper and mix well. Griddle the courgettes for 2–3 minutes on each side until charred and tender. Place onto a serving dish and set aside.

2. Griddle the chillies for 4–5 minutes until charred and soft. Leave to cool. When cool to the touch, remove the skin, deseed and cut into thin strips.

3. Meanwhile, mix the yogurt, garlic, lemon and a good pinch of salt and black pepper in a mixing bowl. Spoon over the courgettes.

4. To serve, arrange the chillies and walnuts over the salad. Crumble over the feta and scatter over the dill. Serve immediately.

Haricot, Egg, Spring Onion and Tahini Salad

Dried beans are sold at food markets throughout Turkey, with enormous sackfuls lining the aisles of the old markets. The tops of the sacks are rolled down to display the beans, so that shoppers can scoop out what they need. Beans are used in a variety of soups, stews and salads. This white bean and egg salad was inspired by the classic Turkish recipe *fasulye piyazi*, where white beans are served with herbs, eggs and olive oil. I have added a richer dressing, using a little tahini. This salad works beautifully with grilled fish or as part of a *meze*.

2 eggs
2 x 400g tins haricot beans, drained and rinsed
5 spring onions, finely sliced
2 handfuls of finely chopped flat-leaf parsley leaves
1 teaspoon Turkish pepper flakes

For the dressing
1 tablespoon olive oil
2 tablespoons tahini paste
juice of ½ lemon
1 teaspoon runny honey
2 tablespoons water
sea salt

Serves 4

1. Cook the eggs in a pan of boiling water for 8–9 minutes until just hard. Cool in cold water, remove the shells and roughly slice the eggs.

2. Meanwhile, whisk the ingredients for the dressing together along with 2 tablespoons of cold water and a good pinch of salt. The tahini will look like it has split, but keep whisking and it will come back together into a rich, creamy dressing.

3. Put the beans, spring onions, parsley and Turkish pepper flakes into a bowl. Pour over the dressing and toss together. Add the sliced eggs and gently fold together. Serve immediately.

Freekeh, Pomegranate and Black Olive Salad

Freekeh, or *firik* in Turkish, is an ancient wholegrain that has been used across the Middle East for centuries. It is a young green wheat that is dried and smoked, giving it a distinctive flavour. In Turkey, it is eaten in *pilav* with vegetables or just cooked with bulgur and lots of butter. I have used this nutty grain for the base of this Turkish-inspired salad, combining it with the classic flavours of pomegranate, Turkish pepper flakes, olives, tomatoes and dill.

200g freekeh
2 tablespoons olive oil
juice of 1 lemon
3 tablespoons pomegranate molasses
½ teaspoon Turkish pepper flakes
5 spring onions, finely sliced
100g pitted black olives, roughly torn
55g sun-dried tomatoes
40g cornichons, finely chopped
2 handfuls of finely chopped dill
30g pomegranate seeds
sea salt and freshly ground black pepper

Serves 4

1. Cook the freekeh according to the packet instructions until tender. Drain, refresh with cold water, and drain again.

2. Meanwhile, mix the oil, lemon juice, pomegranate molasses, Turkish pepper flakes and a good pinch of salt and black pepper together in a small bowl.

3. Put the cooked freekeh in a bowl and add the spring onions, olives, sun-dried tomatoes, cornichons and dill. Pour over the dressing, mix everything together thoroughly and transfer to a serving dish. Top with the pomegranate seeds and serve immediately.

Wild Rice, Kale, Chilli and Pomegranate Salad

This hearty salad is a very modern recipe that is packed with superfoods and classic Turkish ingredients. I love the combination of the mixed rice – using black, red, brown and white gives the salad a variety of colours, textures and flavours. Turkish staples dill, parsley, mint, pomegranate seeds and walnuts add flavour, and the addition of kale gives it a light, modern twist. The dressing uses sumac to give an extra sour note. A little pinch of this ground red berry is a lovely way to introduce more depth of flavour to any salad dressing.

350g mix of black, red, brown and white rice
150g kale
a handful of finely chopped dill
2 handfuls of finely chopped flat-leaf parsley leaves
a handful of finely chopped mint leaves
1 red chilli, deseeded and finely chopped
200g pomegranate seeds
55g walnuts, lightly crushed

For the dressing
4 tablespoons olive oil
3 tablespoons pomegranate molasses
juice of 1 lemon
1 teaspoon caster sugar
1 teaspoon of sumac
sea salt and freshly ground black pepper

Serves 4–6

1. Cook the rice in a large pan of boiling water according to packet instructions, starting with the variety that takes the longest and adding the rest at appropriate times so that they all cook perfectly. Drain and rinse under cold running water. Set aside to drain.

2. Meanwhile, cook the kale for 2–3 minutes in a large pan of boiling water. Drain and refresh under cold running water. When cold, drain thoroughly and squeeze out the excess water with your hands.

3. Whisk all the dressing ingredients together in a small bowl.

4. Put the drained rice in a large mixing bowl and add the kale, herbs, chilli and half the pomegranate seeds and walnuts. Pour in three-quarters of the dressing and mix everything together thoroughly.

5. Tip the salad onto a serving dish and pour over the remaining dressing. Top with the remaining pomegranate seeds and walnuts and serve immediately.

Griddled Aubergines with Saffron Yogurt

During the Ottoman Empire, the city of Safranbolu, between Ankara and the Black Sea, was flourishing. It was located on the Silk Road that linked the east with the western trade routes. The city was was one of the principle growers and traders of saffron, and took its name from this illustrious spice. Today the beautiful town still grows some of the finest saffron in the world, and it is used to flavour stews and desserts throughout Turkey. I have used it here to enrich a simple yogurt dressing, imparting its vibrant yellow colour and slightly musty smell. The dressing is generously poured over grilled aubergines, which are then showered with pomegranate seeds for a slight tang.

2 aubergines, sliced into 5mm rounds
8 tablespoons olive oil
30ml full-fat milk
a pinch of saffron
100g Greek yogurt
1 tablespoon tahini paste
juice of ½ lemon
2 handfuls of finely chopped dill leaves
80g pomegranate seeds
20g pine nuts, toasted
sea salt and freshly ground black pepper

Serves 4

1. Heat a griddle pan over a high heat. Place the aubergines in a shallow dish and pour over the oil. Toss well so that they all get coated in the oil. When the pan is smoking hot, cook the aubergines for 4–5 minutes on each side, or until beautifully charred and tender. Transfer the aubergines to a serving dish.

2. Meanwhile, pour the milk into a microwaveable dish and heat for a few seconds until warm. Sprinkle in the saffron and stir gently with a teaspoon. Leave for a few minutes to infuse.

3. Tip the yogurt into a mixing bowl and add the tahini, lemon juice and a good pinch of salt and black pepper. Pour over the infused saffron milk and mix everything together thoroughly.

4. To serve, drizzle the sunshine-yellow yogurt over the aubergines. Scatter over the dill, pomegranate seeds and pine nuts. Serve immediately with any remaining yogurt on the side.

Fried Halloumi with Herby Salsa

Given the close proximity to Greece, it should come as no surprise that halloumi is eaten as a *meze* dish on the western coast of Turkey and in the modern restaurants of Istanbul. It is often served pan-fried with a tangy tomato salsa. This light and refreshing dish is perfect for a summer's evening. The halloumi must be served straight out of the pan so that it is still hot and oozy when you bite into it. Make sure you have your salsa ready first, so that you can pour it straight over the cooked cheese.

½ red onion, roughly chopped
150g cherry tomatoes
a handful of roughly chopped flat-leaf parsley leaves
a handful of roughly chopped mint leaves
4 tablespoons olive oil
2 tablespoons pomegranate molasses
a pinch of Turkish pepper flakes
500g halloumi, cut into 5mm slices
sea salt and freshly ground black pepper

Serves 4

1. Put the onion into a mini food processor and blend until finely chopped. Add the tomatoes and pulse to create a salsa. Transfer to a mixing bowl and add the herbs, half the oil, the pomegranate molasses, Turkish pepper flakes and a good pinch of salt and black pepper. Mix together thoroughly.

2. Heat the remaining oil in a large frying pan over a medium heat. Fry the halloumi for 1–2 minutes on each side until golden and oozing. Place onto a serving dish and top with the salsa. Serve immediately.

Herby Chicken and Pearl Barley Salad

This light and modern salad is packed with goodness. The base of the salad looks like a colourful slaw, using a classic Turkish combination of red cabbage, carrot, onion and fresh herbs. A tangy yogurt dressing binds it all together beautifully without feeling too creamy. It is perfect to make if you have leftover roast chicken and works brilliantly for a packed lunch or picnic as everything stays crunchy.

250g cooked pearl barley
180g red cabbage, finely sliced
1 carrot, grated
1 red onion, finely sliced
a handful of roughly chopped
flat-leaf parsley leaves
a handful of roughly chopped
mint leaves
juice of ½ lemon
2 tablespoons olive oil
300g roast chicken, shredded
sea salt and freshly ground
black pepper

For the dressing
100g Greek yogurt
50g mayonnaise
juice of ½ lemon

Serves 4

1. Put the pearl barley, cabbage, carrot, onion, parsley and mint into a mixing bowl. Add the lemon juice, oil and a good pinch of salt and black pepper. Mix well.

2. Place all the dressing ingredients in a small bowl along with 2 tablespoons of cold water and season with salt and black pepper. Whisk together to form a smooth mixture.

3. To serve, spread the barley mix onto a large serving plate. Arrange the shredded chicken over the top and drizzle over the dressing. Serve immediately.

Seared Tuna, Orange and Caper Salad

Sitting in the sunshine at a tiny restaurant in the fishing village of Göcek, we were given the catch of the day, gently fried and served with a herby salad in a light orange dressing. It was perfect – the food, my family and the view of the wooden *gulets* sailing in between the islands of the beautiful turquoise bay. It inspired me to create my own version, using pan-fried tuna, masses of fresh herbs, capers and a zingy orange vinaigrette. This recipe also calls for sumac, made from a tart red berry, which gives a sour dimension to the finished salad.

4 tablespoons olive oil
2 tuna steaks (about 120g each)
juice of ½ an orange
juice of ½ a lemon
1 teaspoon English mustard
1 teaspoon caster sugar
a handful of finely chopped dill leaves
a handful of roughly chopped flat-leaf parsley leaves
4 spring onions, finely chopped
1 tablespoon capers, drained
20g pine nuts, toasted
a pinch of sumac
sea salt and freshly ground black pepper

Serves 2

1. Heat half the oil in a large frying pan over a high heat. Add the tuna steaks and sear each side for 30–60 seconds until charred and pink in the middle. Remove from the pan and set aside to cool. Chop the tuna into tiny pieces and transfer to a mixing bowl.

2. To make the dressing, whisk together the remaining olive oil with the orange juice, lemon juice, mustard, sugar and a good pinch of salt and black pepper.

3. Add the herbs, spring onions, capers and pine nuts to the tuna and pour over the dressing. Tip into a serving bowl. Scatter over the sumac and serve immediately.

Baby Octopus, Tomato, Olive and Oregano Salad

Octopus is a classic Aegean *meze* dish that is served with glasses of cold *raki* and plenty of bread. Traditionally, the octopus is cooked until tender, chopped up with green olives and herbs, and served with lemon juice and olive oil. I have slightly refined this, using griddled baby octopus and plenty of fragrant oregano, invoking the scent of the hills that surround this stunning part of Turkey. The simple list of fresh ingredients is so indicative of the cooking of this region, where it's all about using the best produce you can find.

3 tomatoes, roughly chopped
½ red onion, roughly chopped
100g green pitted olives, roughly halved
2 handfuls of roughly torn flat-leaf parsley leaves
a handful of oregano leaves
juice of 1 lemon
2 tablespoons olive oil
300g baby octopus, cleaned and trimmed
sea salt and freshly ground black pepper

Serves 4

1. Put the tomatoes, onion, olives, parsley, oregano, half the lemon juice, 1 tablespoon of the oil and a good pinch of salt and black pepper into a mixing bowl. Toss together and set aside for a few minutes so that the flavours develop.

2. Heat a griddle pan over a high heat. Put the octopus into a mixing bowl with the rest of the oil and season with salt and black pepper. Mix well. Griddle for 1½–2 minutes on each side, until light pink. Place on top of the salad and squeeze over the rest of the lemon juice. Serve immediately.

chapter

6

meat

Lamb is Turkey's most popular meat, from stews to sizzling kebabs.

There are some delicious chicken dishes and beautiful beef recipes, but traditionally, lamb holds centre stage. In nomadic culture, sheep were easy to care for and herd, and lamb was used for everything from simple stews to stuffed dolma, *köfte* and kebabs. My Café Lala Lamb Güvec (see page 159) is a beautifully subtle lamb stew made with aubergines, garlic and tomatoes. It is perfect peasant food and utterly divine.

When it comes to beef, the Turkish have perfected the curing process, making spicy *sujuk* and smoky pastrami to last the long winter months. These cured meats are used in lots of dishes to add a strong, savoury flavour. *Sujuk* is a bit like a chorizo, meaty and spicy, but made with less fat. It is great on *pide*

and with eggs. Turkish pastrami is very smoky and a little chewy, similar to a good-quality Parma ham. It is served in generous quantities with eggs, on *pide*, in borek and finely chopped into *dolma*.

Chicken is popular, too – from tempting Charred Sumac and Oregaono Chicken Wings (see page 140) to Lemon and Apricot Cinnamon Chicken (see page 148), a delicate Ottoman stew that is still popular in Turkey today.

Classic Turkish meals involve charred kebabs, well-seasoned grilled *köfte* and delicately flavoured stews left to cook for hours. The Turkish way with meat has had a huge influence on my cooking style, and these dishes have real staying power.

Charred Sumac and Oregano Chicken Wings

Tavuk kanat, or chicken wings, are barbecued and served all over Turkey, expertly marinated in fragrant herbs and spices. I have used a traditional Turkish marinade made with Turkish pepper flakes, sumac, cumin, oregano and yogurt. The yogurt helps to tenderise the meat and bind all the flavours together. These charred chicken wings are ideal served with the Orange and Celeriac Salad on page 121 and plenty of bread to mop up all the juices.

1kg chicken wings, each wing cut into 2 pieces and trimmed
2 teaspoons Turkish pepper flakes
1 teaspoon sumac
½ teaspoon ground cumin
1 teaspoon dried oregano
2 tablespoons Greek yogurt
2 tablespoons olive oil
2 tablespoons vegetable oil
sea salt

Serves 4

1. Put the chicken wings into a mixing bowl and add the Turkish pepper flakes, sumac, cumin, oregano and a good pinch of salt. Add the yogurt and pour in the olive oil. Mix well, cover and leave to marinate overnight in the fridge.

2. Preheat the oven to 200°C/gas mark 6 and take the chicken wings out of the fridge to come to room temperature. Oil a griddle pan with a little vegetable oil and set over a high heat until smoking hot. Cook the chicken wings for 3–4 minutes on each side until charred and then transfer to a roasting tin. Roast for 12–15 minutes until cooked through. Serve immediately.

Chicken and Orzo Soup

Originating from the town of Manisa on the west coast, this is the Turkish version of the elixir-like Jewish chicken soup, and is a typical winter dish. A whole bird is cooked slowly until tender and shredded into a simple lemony broth. The recipe calls for orzo, small, rice-shaped pieces of pasta that cook really quickly. In Turkey, orzo is used in soups, stews and salads. It is also the base for a simple *pilav*, fried in butter until it turns dark brown, then combined with rice and cooked until both are tender. It gives a really nutty flavour and soft texture to the dish.

1 whole chicken, skinned
½ lemon, plus the juice of 1½
1 onion, peeled and halved
1 garlic bulb, cut in half horizontally
a handful of flat-leaf parsley leaves and stalks
100g butter
3 tablespoons red pepper paste
2 tablespoons tomato purée
300g orzo
sea salt

Serves 6–8

1. Place the chicken in a large saucepan. Add the ½ lemon, onion, garlic and parsley. Cover with 3.5 litres of cold water and bring to the boil over a high heat. Cover, reduce the heat to low and cook gently for 1½ hours, or until the chicken is cooked through. Reserving the cooking water (stock), remove the chicken and set aside to cool. Pull off the breasts – you won't need them for the soup, so save them for a sandwich. Pick off the rest of the meat, discarding any bones, and set aside.

2. Heat the butter in a large saucepan over a medium heat. Add the red pepper paste and tomato purée. Whisk in a little stock to loosen, then slowly pour in all but 500ml of the stock (you can discard the rest, or keep it for another recipe) and whisk together. Add the lemon juice and a large pinch of salt. Bring to the boil and add the orzo. Cover, reduce the heat to low and cook for 10–12 minutes until the orzo is tender.

3. Tip the shredded chicken into the soup and mix well. Cook, stirring occasionally, for 5 minutes or until the chicken has reheated. Remove from the heat, cover and leave for 5 minutes for the flavours to develop, then serve immediately.

Konya Chicken Sandwich

Konya, in the Central Anatolian region, has some of the best street food in Turkey. On every corner there is something delicious to be found: a crispy syrup-soaked doughnut here, a *tandir* kebab there. My favourite type of Konya street food, though, has to be the chicken sandwich that can be bought from a hole-in-the-wall called Merisin Tantuni: beautifully cooked, spiced chicken, served in a chicken-juice-soaked bap, stuffed with filling. The version I've recreated below may be a little more refined, but the essence is still very much there.

1 large baguette
2 tablespoons olive oil
400g roast chicken, shredded
2 tablespoons red pepper paste
1 teaspoon freshly ground black pepper
½ teaspoon ground cumin
a handful of roughly chopped flat-leaf parsley leaves
juice of ½ lemon
sea salt

To serve
8 tablespoons mayonnaise
2 tomatoes, sliced
1 red onion, finely sliced
1 baby lettuce, sliced

Serves 4

1. Preheat the oven to 180°/gas mark 4. Slice the baguette open and put in the oven for 4–5 minutes until warmed through.

2. Meanwhile, heat the oil in a frying pan over a high heat. Add the chicken and leave for 1 minute so that it starts to colour. Mix the red pepper paste with 100ml of cold water and pour it over the chicken. Add the black pepper, cumin and a good pinch of salt. Mix together thoroughly and fry for 2–3 minutes until heated through. Add the parsley and lemon juice and mix well.

3. To serve, spread the mayonnaise over the baguette. Layer over the tomatoes, onion and lettuce. Top generously with the chicken, close the baguette and slice it into four pieces. Serve immediately with a cold beer.

Spiced Chicken and Bulgur *Pilav* with a Crunchy Walnut Topping

2 tablespoons olive oil
1 tablespoon butter
1 onion, finely chopped
2 Turkish green peppers, deseeded and finely sliced
2 tomatoes, peeled and finely chopped
2 tablespoons tomato purée
1 tablespoon red pepper paste
½ teaspoon freshly ground black pepper
275g bulgur wheat
550ml boiling water
sea salt

For the walnut topping
1 tablespoon butter
1 tablespoon olive oil
100g walnuts, finely crushed
1 teaspoon Turkish pepper flakes
½ teaspoon ground cumin
¼ teaspoon freshly ground black pepper

For the chicken
2 tablespoons olive oil
500g chicken breasts, thinly sliced
1 tablespoon tomato purée
½ teaspoon Turkish pepper flakes
½ teaspoon freshly ground black pepper
½ teaspoon dried mint

A few years ago my friend Fatma taught me to make this *pilav* at her apartment in Adana, using a recipe her mother had taught her. It's an impressive dish: nutty bulgur *pilav*, tender stripes of chicken and a spicy walnut topping, with a slight hint of sweetness from the cinnamon.

Serves 4

1. Heat the oil and butter in a pan over a medium heat. Add the onion and green peppers and cook, stirring occasionally, for 5–6 minutes until soft. Add the tomatoes and cook, stirring occasionally, for 1–2 minutes until they start to break down. Add the tomato purée, red pepper paste, black pepper and a good pinch of salt. Mix well and add the bulgur and the boiling water. Stir, cover and reduce the heat to low. Simmer for 20 minutes, or until the bulgur is tender and all the water absorbed.

2. Meanwhile, make the walnut topping. Heat the butter and olive oil in a small saucepan. Add the walnuts and fry for 2–3 minutes until they smell really nutty. Stir in the Turkish pepper flakes, cumin, black pepper and a pinch of salt. Remove from the heat, then transfer to a cold plate to cool down before using.

3. For the chicken, heat the oil in a large, non-stick frying pan over a high heat. Add the chicken and fry for 5–6 minutes until just cooked through. Add the tomato purée, Turkish pepper flakes, black pepper and mint. Stir and continue to fry for 1–2 minutes until everything is coated.

4. To serve, tip the bulgur onto a large serving plate. Spoon over the chicken and sprinkle over the walnuts. Serve immediately.

Balli Mahmudiye – Lemon and Apricot Cinnamon Chicken

During the 15th and 16th centuries, a dish called *Balli Mahmudiye* was served at opulent dinner parties in the Ottoman capital of Bursa. Originally named after Sultan Mahmud, it was a lavish mix of chicken cooked with apples, raisins, currants, apricots, almonds and pine nuts – it was a real celebration of ingredients and wealth. Still cooked in Turkish restaurants today, *Balli mahmudiye* is often toned down with a shorter list of fruit and nuts, but retains the same light, lemony sauce. My recipe uses orzo, which is somewhat lighter than rice and complements the sweet flavours of the cinnamon and apricots beautifully.

300g orzo

2 tablespoons butter

a handful of finely chopped flat-leaf parsley leaves

a handful of finely chopped dill

1 teaspoon Turkish pepper flakes

4 tablespoons olive oil

600g skinless chicken breasts, cut into strips

1 onion, finely chopped

55g blanched almonds

100g dried apricots, roughly sliced

juice of 2 lemons

1 teaspoon runny honey

½ teaspoon ground cinnamon

1 teaspoon freshly ground black pepper

2–3 tablespoons boiling water

1 teaspoon cornflour

sea salt

Serves 4

1. Cook the orzo in a pan of boiling water according to the packet instructions. Drain and return to the pan. Add the butter and a generous pinch of salt. Stir in the herbs and Turkish pepper flakes.

2. Heat the oil in a large pan over a high heat and add the chicken. Fry for 2–3 minutes to seal the meat. Add the onion and almonds and fry for a further 3–4 minutes until golden.

3. Reduce the heat to medium and add the apricots, lemon juice, honey, cinnamon, black pepper and a generous pinch of salt. Add the boiling water and continue to cook for 1–2 minutes. Add the cornflour and mix together until thickened. Serve immediately with the orzo.

Chicken Stuffed with Spinach and Cheese

This is a modern Turkish recipe that is rather reminiscent of Cordon Bleu Chicken. The stuffed chicken breasts are cooked slowly in spiced milk, which keeps the chicken beautifully tender and imparts the flavours of the garlic, black pepper and dried mint. The classic recipe would use a soft, stringy Turkish cheese such as *lor peyniri*, which oozes out of the chicken and thickens the sauce. In this recipe I have used mozzarella – it is easier to come by, has the same milkiness and melts beautifully into the sauce.

4 tablespoons olive oil
250g spinach
200g grated mozzarella cheese
1 garlic clove, crushed
30g pine nuts
4 chicken breasts, flattened with a rolling pin
sea salt and freshly ground black pepper

For the sauce
250ml full-fat milk
1 tablespoons red pepper paste
1 tablespoon tomato purée
1 garlic clove, crushed
1 teaspoon freshly ground black pepper
½ teaspoon dried mint

Serves 4

1. Heat half the oil in a large frying pan over a high heat and add the spinach. Fry for 1–2 minutes until wilted. Transfer to a mixing bowl and use the back of a spoon to squeeze out any excess moisture and pour away. Add the mozzarella, garlic, pine nuts and a good pinch of salt and pepper. Mix together thoroughly.

2. Lay the chicken on a chopping board. Place a quarter of the spinach in a line down the centre of each chicken breast. Pull up one side of the meat and roll over. Fasten with cocktail sticks and place into a shallow ovenproof dish.

3. To make the sauce, whisk all the ingredients together in a mixing bowl. Pour over the chicken. Cover and marinate in the fridge for 30 minutes.

4. Preheat the oven to 180°C/gas mark 4. Drizzle the remaining oil over the chicken and roast for 30–35 minutes, or until the chicken is cooked through and the sauce really thick. Serve immediately.

Granny's *Pilav*

My lovely Turkish mum, Tülay, introduced me to the joys of *içli pilav* several years ago. It is a hearty rice dish made with shredded chicken, chicken hearts, livers and lots of nuts and dried fruit. Originally from Mardin in eastern Turkey, the dish is decadent and rooted in *meyhane* culture – *içli pilav* was served in taverns to the men of the town, along with glasses of chilled *raki*. The recipe uses lots of allspice and black pepper, which gives the dish its distinctive taste and strong smell, but I've left out the chicken hearts.

175g chicken livers
1 chicken breast (about 125g)
2 tablespoons butter
1 tablespoon olive oil
1 onion, finely chopped
25g pine nuts
40g raisins
2½ teaspoons dried mint
1½ teaspoons allspice
1 teaspoon freshly ground black pepper
1 teaspoon caster sugar
300g basmati rice
700ml hot chicken stock
sea salt

Serves 4

1. Put the chicken livers and breast in a pan of water and bring to the boil over a high heat. Remove any scum and add a generous pinch of salt. Reduce the heat to low and simmer for 10–15 minutes, or until the chicken is cooked through. Drain and leave to cool. Once cool, finely slice the livers and shred the chicken. Set to one side.

2. Heat the butter and oil in a large pan over a medium heat. Add the onion and pine nuts and cook, stirring occasionally, for 6–7 minutes, or until the pine nuts are golden. Add the raisins, mint, allspice, black pepper, sugar and cooked chicken liver and breast. Add a generous pinch of salt and mix everything thoroughly.

3. Tip the rice into the pan and mix for a minute until the rice turns translucent. Pour in the stock and stir gently. Cover, reduce the heat to low and cook for 20–25 minutes, or until the rice is really full and tender. Remove from the heat and cover with a clean tea towel. Put the lid back on and leave for 10 minutes. This will help the rice fluff up. Fork onto a serving dish and serve immediately.

Arnavut Cigeri – Liver, Onions and Sumac

I first tasted *arnavut cigeri* at Karaköy lokantası in Istanbul, a stunning art deco restaurant near the Bosphorus. This luscious liver recipe is a favourite across Turkey. The liver is cooked gently until it is meltingly tender, and seasoned with sumac, Turkish pepper flakes and a very subtle dusting of cumin. This dish is always served with lemon, parsley and sweet red onions.

2 red onions, finely sliced
juice of 1 lemon
1 teaspoon sumac
600g calves' liver, cut into
10–12cm strips
2 tablespoons butter
½ teaspoon Turkish
pepper flakes
½ teaspoon ground cumin
small handful of finely chopped
flat-leaf parsley leaves,
sea salt and freshly ground
black pepper
lemon wedges, to serve

Serves 4

1. Put the onions into a mixing bowl. Add half the lemon juice, the sumac and a good pinch of salt. Mix together thoroughly and set aside.

2. Put the liver in a mixing bowl and season with a generous pinch of salt and black pepper and mix well.

3. Heat the butter in a frying pan over a medium heat until bubbling. Add the liver and cook gently, shaking the pan occasionally, for 1½–2 minutes. Turn the liver, reduce the heat to low and cook for another 1½–2 minutes, or until golden and still a little pink in the centre.

4. Add the Turkish pepper flakes, cumin and the remaining lemon juice. Give the pan a really good shake. Remove from the heat and scatter over the parsley. Serve immediately with the onions and lemon wedges for squeezing.

Beef, Okra and Lemon Stew

This recipe is inspired by *bamya çorbası*, a sour Anatolian soup made with lemon and okra. Traditionally prepared for weddings, the tangy flavour of this soup meant it was served as a palate cleanser in between the main course and dessert. I have used a traditional recipe but left out most of the liquid, so that you have a thick sauce rather than a broth. The recipe uses lots of lemon juice and dried mint, classic Turkish flavours that work beautifully with beef and really lighten up what would otherwise be quite a heavy dish.

2 tablespoons olive oil
500g stewing beef, cut into bite-sized pieces
2 onions, finely chopped
2 tablespoons tomato purée
2 tablespoons red pepper paste
juice of 2 lemons and grated zest of ½ lemon
300ml boiling water
350g okra, topped and halved lengthways
1½ tablespoons butter
½ teaspoon dried mint
sea salt and freshly ground black pepper

Serves 4

1. Heat the oil in a large pan over a high heat. Add the beef and cook for 5–6 minutes, stirring occasionally, until browned. Reduce the heat to medium and add the onions. Mix well and cook, stirring occasionally, for 3–4 minutes until soft.

2. Add the tomato purée, red pepper paste, the juice of ½ lemon and a good pinch of salt and pepper. Pour in the boiling water and stir together. Cover, reduce the heat to low and cook for 1 hour until the beef is just tender.

3. Meanwhile, add the juice of 1 lemon to a small pan of boiling water. Add the okra and cook for 3–4 minutes to stop them going sticky. Drain and refresh under cold running water and set aside.

4. Tip the okra into the beef stew and mix together. Cover and cook for 20–25 minutes, or until the okra is lovely and tender.

5. Heat the butter in a small pan over a medium heat until bubbling. Add the mint and lemon zest. Swirl together, then pour over the cooked stew. Add the remaining lemon juice, mix everything together and serve immediately.

Café Lala Lamb Güveç

As I travelled across the plains of Anatolia, on my way from Konya to the Aegean coast, I passed through the sleepy village of Ilgın. Here, in her little restaurant, Saliha taught me how to cook a few local dishes. It was freezing and we huddled around her stove as we cooked. I loved this simple stew, cooked to perfection with only a few ingredients in an old earthenware pot. Everything cooks separately in layers, which are then mixed together right at the end. If you don't have an earthenware pot, use a heavy-based casserole dish instead.

500g lamb neck fillets
2 tablespoons olive oil
2 tablespoons red pepper paste
1 tablespoon tomato purée
8 aubergines, half skinned so that they are stripy, and cut into 2.5cm rounds
4 Turkish green peppers, deseeded and sliced
1 garlic bulb, cloves separated, peeled and roughly chopped
400g tin chopped tomatoes
sea salt and freshly ground black pepper

Serves 4

1. Put the lamb in a saucepan and pour over 1 litre of cold water. Cover and cook over a medium heat for 1 hour, or until cooked through. Drain, reserving the stock, and place the lamb in the bottom of an oiled casserole dish. Heat over a medium–high heat, stirring occasionally, for 3–4 minutes, or until golden.

2. Meanwhile, preheat the oven to 200°C/gas mark 6 and mix 100ml of the stock with the red pepper paste and tomato purée, then whisk in 750ml of the stock.

3. Put the aubergines on top of the lamb and then add the green peppers, garlic and finally the tomatoes. Pour over the mixed stock. Cover and cook in the oven for 1½–2 hours until the tomatoes have formed a thick sauce and the lamb is beautifully tender. When you take the stew out of the oven, it can look quite dry, but mix it together and it will turn into a wonderfully thick stew. Serve immediately.

Güveçte Kuzu Incik –
Ottoman Lamb Shank Stew

In the Ottoman kitchens, *Güveçte Kuzu Incik* would have been cooked in huge pots until tender and served with *pilav* bejewelled with fruit. This opulent stew is light and herby and the meat falls off the bone. It is delicious served with a crisp green salad and bread.

2 tablespoons olive oil

4 lamb shanks, about 400–500g each

1 onion, finely chopped

1 carrot, finely chopped

2 celery stalks, finely chopped

4 garlic cloves, thinly sliced

400g tin chopped tomatoes

2 tablespoons tomato purée

½ teaspoon caster sugar

2 rosemary sprigs

3 bay leaves

juice of ½ lemon

500ml boiling water

sea salt and freshly ground black pepper

Serves 4

1. Preheat the oven to 180°C/gas mark 4. Heat the oil in large casserole dish over a medium–high heat and add the lamb shanks, two at a time. Cook for 6–8 minutes, turning the shanks so that they brown on all sides. Remove from the pan and set aside.

2. Reheat the pan over a low–medium heat and add the onion, carrot and celery. Mix well and cook, stirring occasionally, for 7–8 minutes, or until soft. Add the garlic, mix well and cook for 10 seconds until fragrant.

3. Tip the tomatoes into the pan and add the tomato purée, sugar, rosemary, bay leaves, lemon juice and a good pinch of salt and black pepper. Pour in the boiling water and mix everything together thoroughly. Return the lamb shanks to the pan, making sure the meat is three-quarters covered in the sauce. Cover and cook in the oven for 2–2½ hours (check every 15 minutes after 2 hours), or until the lamb falls off the bone at the touch of a fork. Serve immediately.

Denizli Aubergine *Dolma*

Denizli is an industrial town in western Anatolia, surrounded by huge mountains. My partner and I stopped at a café there, where we dined on stuffed aubergine *dolma* and fresh salads. The original recipe used dried aubergines. These are hollowed out, dried in the summer sun and threaded onto string. They hang like beautiful necklaces ready for the winter. Dried aubergines are hard to find outside of Turkey so I use fresh aubergines when I can't get them. Sadly, this means that the flesh is scooped out and not used. Rather than throw it away, I suggest mixing the cooked aubergine flesh with a little lemon juice, olive oil and salt and pepper to serve as a side dish to the *dolma*.

6 tablespoons olive oil
3 aubergines, cut in half lengthways and flat sides scored into a criss-cross pattern
1 onion, finely chopped
250g lamb mince
160g basmati rice
2 tablespoons red pepper paste
2 tablespoons tomato purée
1½ teaspoons Turkish pepper flakes
1 teaspoon ground black pepper
350ml boiling water
a handful of finely chopped flat-leaf parsley leaves
1 garlic clove, finely chopped
sea salt
Greek yogurt, to serve

Serves 6

1. Preheat the oven to 200°C/gas mark 6. Drizzle ½ teaspoon of the oil over each halved aubergine and place on a roasting tray. Cook in the oven for 30–35 minutes, or until soft and a little golden. Remove from the oven and leave to cool. When cool to the touch, carefully scoop out most of the flesh and keep to one side in a bowl to use as you like (see above). Put the aubergine shells back into the roasting tray.

2. Meanwhile, heat 2 tablespoons of the oil in a pan over a medium heat. Add the onion and cook, stirring occasionally, for 3–4 minutes until a little golden. Add the lamb and fry for 2–3 minutes until cooked through.

3. Add the rice, red pepper paste, tomato purée, Turkish pepper flakes, black pepper and boiling water. Mix together, cover and reduce the heat to low. Cook for 12–15 minutes until the rice is tender. Remove from the heat and leave for 5 minutes to fluff up. Season with a good pinch of salt and fork in the parsley.

4. Carefully spoon the rice into the cooked aubergines. Scatter over the garlic and drizzle the remaining oil over the top. Pop the stuffed aubergines into the oven for 5–6 minutes to allow the rice to take on some of the aubergine flavour. Serve immediately with yogurt.

Mevlana *Pilav*

Mevlana pilavi was created in the kitchens of the 13th century philosopher Mevlana. It was a celebratory dish that was a real showstopper. Traditionally, the recipe called for lamb, black pepper, carrots, onion and chestnuts, all cooked until tender and then forked apart. The chestnuts were boiled until soft, then peeled, roughly chopped and added to the rice. I find that they are too bitter, so I have left them out. But if you want to be a purist, you can add the prepared chestnuts to the cooked *pilav* as they did all those years ago.

750g shoulder of lamb on the
bone, cut into 7.5–10cm pieces
2 tablespoons olive oil
½ onion, finely sliced
1 carrot, cut in half and
finely sliced
300g basmati rice
30g raisins
25g pine nuts
1 teaspoon ground cinnamon
1 teaspoon freshly ground
black pepper
2 handfuls of finely chopped
flat-leaf parsley leaves
sea salt

Serves 4

1. Put the lamb in a pan and cover with 2 litres of cold water. Bring to the boil over a high heat. Cover, reduce the heat to low and cook for 1–1½ hours, or until tender. Remove the lamb from the pan and leave to cool. Reserve the stock. When cool enough to handle, discard the bones and fat and shred the meat.

2. Heat the oil in a large pan over a medium heat and add the onion and carrot. Mix well and fry, stirring occasionally, for 5–6 minutes until soft.

3. Add the shredded lamb and cook, stirring occasionally, for 3–4 minutes to take on a little colour. Add the rice, raisins, pine nuts, cinnamon, black pepper and a pinch of salt.

4. Pour in 700ml of the reserved stock and stir together. Cover, reduce the heat to low and cook for 15 minutes until the stock has been absorbed and the rice is tender. Remove from the heat and cover with a clean tea towel. Cover with the lid and leave for 10 minutes. This will help the rice fluff up. Fork onto a serving dish. Scatter over the parsley and serve immediately.

Sac Kavurma – Smoky Fried Lamb with Peppers, Tomatoes and Garlic

In Turkish this is *Sac Kavurma* – 'sac' meaning 'iron plate', which is the basis of this dish and what gives it its intense, smoky flavour. Lamb is cooked with onions and green peppers on a searing hot iron plate and served in the same pan at the table. This dish is made in huge quantities for weddings in the villages that are strewn across the mountains of eastern Turkey. To achieve a similar flavour at home, I use a wok that is heated until smoking before adding the lamb.

2 tablespoons olive oil
600g lamb topside or fillet steak, thinly sliced
2 onions, roughly chopped
2 Turkish green peppers, roughly sliced
4 garlic cloves, thinly sliced
2 tomatoes, skinned and chopped
1 tablespoon tomato purée
1½ teaspoons Turkish pepper flakes
1 teaspoon freshly ground black pepper
½ teaspoon dried thyme
100ml boiling water
1 tablespoon butter
small handful of finely chopped flat-leaf parsley leaves
sea salt

Serves 4

1. Heat a large wok over a high heat until smoking hot. Add the oil and lamb and stir-fry for 2–3 minutes to sear the meat. Add the onions and stir-fry for a further 2–3 minutes until golden.

2. Add the green peppers and garlic and continue to stir-fry for 2–3 minutes until the peppers are soft. Tip in the tomatoes and stir-fry for 1–2 minutes more so that they start to break down.

3. Add the tomato purée, Turkish pepper flakes, black pepper, thyme, a good pinch of salt and the boiling water. Mix everything together thoroughly and remove from the heat. Add the butter and parsley, mix together and serve immediately.

Black Olive-encrusted Pulled Lamb

Turkish people take great pride in procuring the very best lamb and cooking it to perfection so that it's tender and juicy. One of the classic celebratory dishes in Turkey is a roasted shoulder of lamb called *tandır*. Roasted slowly in a clay oven, the lamb is incredibly moist and flavoured with a few spices once cooked. Living in London, I have fallen for the pulled meat craze, so I decided to introduce this element to the classic *tandır*, along with a black olive crust to bring in the flavours of the Mediterranean. This Anglo-Turkish dish is a real dinner party centrepiece and, with a few added sides, makes the perfect feast.

200g pitted black olives, drained
a large handful of flat-leaf parsley leaves
4 anchovies, drained
2 garlic cloves, crushed
1 teaspoon sumac
1 teaspoon Turkish pepper flakes
2 teaspoons dried oregano
4 tablespoons olive oil, plus a little extra for brushing
juice of 1 lemon
2kg shoulder of lamb, on the bone
sea salt and freshly ground black pepper

Serves 4–6

1. Put the olives, parsley, anchovies, garlic, sumac, Turkish pepper flakes, oregano and oil into a food processor or blender. Add the lemon juice and season with salt and black pepper. Blend into a coarse paste.

2. Put the lamb in a roasting tray. Scoop out the paste and rub it all over the lamb. Cover and refrigerate for 2 hours or overnight.

3. Preheat the oven to 230°C/gas mark 8 and get the meat out of the fridge to come to room temperature. Brush the lamb with a little oil. Pour in 150ml of cold water and cover with wet baking paper. Cover the lamb in foil and place into the oven. Reduce the heat to 170°C/gas mark 3 and roast for 3–3 ½ hours, or until tender. You should be able to stick two forks into the deepest part of the meat and it should pull apart really easily.

4. To serve, scrape off the paste from the surface of the meat and set aside. Discard any fat and fork apart the lamb. Pour off any excess fat from the roasting tray and return the lamb. Add the set aside paste, mix together and serve immediately.

7

seafood

Turkey is surrounded by four seas:

the Black Sea in the north, the Aegean sea in west, the crystal clear Mediterranean Sea in the south and the busy waters of the Sea of Marmara surrounding Istanbul. Seafood is abundant: juicy prawns, *levrek* (sea bass), huge *lüfer* (bluefish), mackerel, turbot, swordfish, large mussels, sardines, *hamsi* (anchovies), octopus and clams.

Balik (fish) restaurants are a fixture on the Turkish dining scene, from small local eateries serving the catch of the day with seasonal vegetables, to the high-end, glamorous *lokantas* of Istanbul, where the jet-setters go for *meze*, fish and chilled *raki*. Seafood is even a key part of Turkish street food – one of the most popular street food snacks are stuffed mussels, which are sold from little carts in every Turkish city.

In most cases, fish is prepared simply in Turkey, often pan-fried with lots of butter or peppery olive oil, and served with fresh rocket, lemon juice and seasonal vegetables. Garlic, bay leaves, black pepper and fresh herbs are used to add extra flavour.

In the north, on the Black Sea, *hamsi* are a talking point. These silvery anchovies have an intense flavour and are cooked in many different ways, from crispy pancakes for breakfast to the intricate *hamsi pilav* for dinner, where the little fish are cleaned, boned and butterflied to line a roasting dish that is filled with *pilav* and baked.

Even away from the coastal areas, seafood forms an important part of the Turkish diet. The huge lakes in the central and eastern regions of Turkey are teeming with fish and in the capital, Ankara, which sits many miles from the coast in Central Anatolia, fresh seafood is brought in daily.

The dishes in this chapter attempt to explore the very best of Turkish seafood: Calamari with *Tarator* Sauce (see page 172) will bring the flavours of the Mediterranean coast to your table, Fisherman's Stew (see page 191) provides a rustic taste of the seaside town of Marmaris, and Salt-baked Sea Bream (see page 186) makes the ultimate dinner party piece.

Calamari with *Tarator* Sauce

The coastal town of Mersin lies near the borders of Syria and Iraq on the south coast of Turkey. On a recent trip there, I stopped off for lunch in the most stunning spot: a little restaurant with ancient ruins crumbling into the hills that surrounded it and a small terrace that looked out to sea. We feasted on the catch of the day and huge plates of crispy calamari with a rich *tarator* sauce, made from bread, garlic, pine nuts and olive oil. The fresh flavours of this dish evoke the Mediterranean.

vegetable oil, for deep-frying
500g squid, washed and cut into 5mm rings
4 tablespoons durum flour
1 teaspoon bicarbonate of soda
½ teaspoon Turkish pepper flakes
sea salt and freshly ground black pepper

For the *tarator* sauce
2 slices of white bread, crusts removed
1 garlic clove, crushed
juice of ½ lemon
2 tablespoons olive oil
225g Greek yogurt
1 tablespoon plus 1 teaspoon tahini paste

Serves 4

1. First, make the sauce. Blend the bread to fine breadcrumbs in a food processor or blender and then tip into a mixing bowl. Add the garlic, lemon juice, oil and 100ml of cold water. Mix together into a paste. Add the yogurt, tahini and a good pinch of salt. Mix everything together really well. Cover and set aside for the flavours to develop.

2. Heat the oil for frying in a deep pan over a medium–high heat. Put the squid into a mixing bowl and add the flour, bicarbonate of soda, Turkish pepper flakes and a good pinch of salt and black pepper. Mix together thoroughly so that the flour forms a paste that sticks to the squid rings.

3. Carefully drop the squid into the oil in batches of 10–12 pieces and fry for 2–3 minutes until golden and crispy. Remove with a slotted spoon and place onto kitchen paper to drain while you fry the rest of the squid. Serve immediately with the *tarator* sauce.

Karides – Prawns with Sun-dried Tomatoes and Butter

Karides are served all over the Aegean and Mediterranean coast of Turkey as an appetiser to grilled fish. This is one of my dad's favourite Turkish dishes. He loves the smoky flavour of the scorched sun-dried tomatoes, and the buttery sauce. I like my prawns really spicy, but if you are not a fan, only add 1 teaspoon of Turkish pepper flakes for a milder flavour. There are many variations of *karides* served across Turkey, some with vegetables and some with a waxy cheese melted over the top.

55g sun-dried tomatoes (not in oil)
4 tablespoons butter
1 tablespoon olive oil
3 garlic cloves, sliced
500g king prawns, shelled
2 teaspoons Turkish pepper flakes
½ teaspoon freshly ground black pepper
juice of ½ lemon
a handful of roughly chopped flat-leaf parsley leaves
sea salt
crusty bread, to serve

Serves 4

1. Heat a frying pan over a high heat and add the sun-dried tomatoes, skin-side down. Cook for 2–3 minutes until blistered. Remove from the heat and set aside to cool. Once cool enough to touch, finely slice.

2. Allow the pan to cool and then reheat over a medium heat and melt the butter and oil together. Add the garlic and cook for 1 minute, then add the prawns and fry for 1–2 minutes until half cooked. Add the sun-dried tomatoes, Turkish pepper flakes, black pepper and a tiny pinch of salt. Fry for a further 1–2 minutes, or until the prawns are coral-coloured and cooked through.

3. Add the lemon juice and parsley, mix together and serve immediately with masses of crusty bread for mopping up the juices.

Scallops with Black Pepper and Thyme

Bozcaada is a small island off the west coast of Turkey that is famous for the tastiest scallops in the country. They pluck them out of the water during the summer months and cook them with a few herbs, black pepper and garlic. Keeping it simple like this is the best approach with scallops, as they are already so full of the fresh flavours of the sea. Get the best scallops that you can, and serve them with a large handful of chopped parsley and plenty of lemon juice to freshen them up at the end.

500g scallops
3 tablespoons olive oil
¼ teaspoon dried thyme
½ teaspoon Turkish pepper flakes
½ teaspoon freshly ground black pepper
juice of ½ lemon
a handful of roughly chopped flat-leaf parsley leaves
sea salt

Serves 4

1. Put the scallops into a mixing bowl and add 1 tablespoon of the oil, along with the thyme, Turkish pepper flakes, black pepper and a pinch of salt. Mix well.

2. Heat the remaining oil in a frying pan over a high heat. Sear the scallops for 1–2 minutes on each side, or until golden and just cooked through.

3. Squeeze over the lemon and add the parsley. Give the pan a good shake and serve immediately.

Trabzon-baked Cod

On a cold, blustery evening in Trabzon on the Black Sea coast, over lots of cold beer and *raki*, my friend İshan made this incredible baked fish for me. In a clay pot, he layered up white fish, onions and a tomato sauce, then simply baked it in the oven – it was effortless. This rustic style of cooking is typical of the Black Sea region. I have taken this simple dish a step further and added olives and slivers of salty preserved lemons. These are not typically Turkish, but I love the way that the flavour of the preserved lemon melts through the finished dish.

2 tablespoons olive oil, plus extra for drizzling
1 onion, finely chopped
2 Turkish green peppers, deseeded and sliced
2 garlic cloves, finely chopped
1 tomato, finely chopped
150ml tomato passata
2 tablespoons red pepper paste
100ml hot water
4 cod steaks (about 150g each)
55g pitted black olives
1 preserved lemon, pith removed, finely sliced
a handful of finely chopped flat-leaf parsley leaves
sea salt and freshly ground black pepper

Serves 4

1. Preheat the oven to 180°C/gas mark 4. Heat the oil in a frying pan over a high heat and add the onion, green peppers and garlic. Fry for 2–3 minutes until golden. Add the tomato, passata, red pepper paste and hot water. Season with salt and black pepper and mix well. Fry for 3–4 minutes until the sauce is nice and thick.

2. Oil a baking dish and arrange the fish over the bottom. Pour over the sauce and scatter over the olives and preserved lemon. Drizzle over a little oil and roast for 15 minutes until the fish is just cooked through. Scatter with the parsley and serve immediately.

Fried Mackerel with Red Cabbage

This simple dish is based on the classic Turkish *balik ekmek*, or fish sandwich, that is served to hungry fishermen along the Bosphorus. Stalls serving *balik ekmek*, with grated salad and plenty of lemon juice, can be found dotted throughout Istanbul. For my version, I keep all the fresh elements of this vibrant street food, minus the bread, and serve the crispy fish with a tangy onion and cabbage salad.

vegetable oil, for shallow-frying
4 mackerel fillets (about 80–100g each)
3 tablespoons yellow cornflour or fine polenta
1 onion, finely sliced
juice of 1 lemon
½ teaspoon sumac
½ red cabbage, finely sliced
sea salt and freshly ground black pepper

Serves 4

1. Heat about 1cm of oil in a frying pan over a medium heat. Put the mackerel into a dish and add the cornflour or polenta. Season with salt and black pepper and mix well so that the fillets are well coated. Carefully drop the fish into the oil, skin-side down, and cook for 4–5 minutes until golden. Flip and cook for a further 2–3 minutes, or until just cooked through and wondrously crispy.

2. Meanwhile, put the onion into a mixing bowl and add half the lemon juice. Add the sumac and a good pinch of salt. Mix well and leave for a few minutes to take out the rawness. Put the red cabbage on a serving dish and squeeze over the remaining lemon. Season with salt and black pepper and mix together.

3. To serve, scatter the onion over the cabbage and top with the golden fish. Serve immediately.

Baked Sea Bass with *Raki*

Baked sea bass is a typically Turkish food. It is served with peppery wild rocket, lemon wedges and plenty of ice-cold *raki*, and makes a great dinner party dish. For this recipe, I have incorporated all these flavours into one dish. The herbs, lemon, peppery seasoning and *raki* all gently flavour the fish without overpowering it – now all you need is good company.

2 onions, finely sliced
2 handfuls of roughly chopped
flat-leaf parsley leaves
2 handfuls of roughly chopped
mint leaves
a handful of roughly
chopped dill
2 teaspoons sumac
1 teaspoon Turkish
pepper flakes
1 teaspoon freshly ground
black pepper
2 lemons, finely sliced
4 sea bass, gutted and cleaned
(about 180g each)
50ml Turkish *raki* or ouzo
2 tablespoons butter
2 tablespoons olive oil
sea salt

Serves 4

1. Preheat the oven to 180°C/gas mark 4.

2. Mix the onions, herbs, sumac, Turkish pepper flakes, black pepper, lemons and a good pinch of salt together in a mixing bowl.

3. Place two of the sea bass on a large sheet of baking paper and stuff the cavities of the fish with a good handful of the herb mixture. Arrange the remainder of the herbs over the top.

4. Pour over the *raki* and dollop the butter over the fish. Drizzle with the oil, then fold up the sides of the baking paper over the fish and wrap tightly. Repeat with the other two fish.

5. Carefully place the parcels on a baking tray and roast for 25–30 minutes, or until just cooked through and beautifully tender and juicy. Serve immediately.

Swordfish, Tomatoes, Lemon and Oregano

Swordfish has such a great flavour and texture: when cooked properly, the tough flesh turns soft and buttery. It is caught in the deep, warm waters that surround much of south-west Turkey, where it is eaten simply grilled or cut into chunks for a kebab. I like to prepare swordfish with lots of garlic and tomatoes and a big herbal hit from a handful of fresh oregano, which smells of the hills that roll down into the sea all over this part of Turkey.

2 tablespoons olive oil
2 bay leaves
4 garlic cloves, finely sliced
4 swordfish steaks (about 120g each)
2 tablespoons butter
4 spring onions, finely sliced
150g cherry tomatoes, halved
½ teaspoon Turkish pepper flakes
juice of ½ lemon
a handful of fresh oregano
sea salt

Serves 4

1. Put the oil, bay leaves and garlic in a large frying pan over a medium heat. Add the swordfish and cook for 3–4 minutes on each side until golden and cooked through. Remove the fish from the pan and place in a serving dish. Cover with foil and set aside.

2. Reheat the pan over a high heat and melt the butter. Add the spring onions, tomatoes, Turkish pepper flakes and a good pinch of salt. Fry for 3–4 minutes until the tomatoes soften a little. Add the lemon juice and oregano and mix together. Pour over the fish and serve immediately.

Salt-baked Sea Bream

This eccentric fish dish is served all along the Aegean coast of Turkey. After plenty of *meze* and *raki*, the sea bream is brought to the table still enrobed in salt. A very strong alcohol is poured over the top and set on fire, before the casing is cracked open and the fish is served. The salt acts as a blanket from the heat of the oven, protecting the fish so that it steams gently in the local flavours of garlic, dill and lemon. Make sure that you use good-quality rock salt for this and buy plenty so that the fish is completely covered. It's really important to leave the fish to stand for a few minutes when you take it out of the oven. This resting time will allow the fish to relax and retain more flavour.

1kg good-quality rock salt
½ tablespoon dried oregano
½ tablespoon dried mint
1 sea bream (about 600g), cleaned and gutted
1 garlic bulb, sliced in half widthways
a large bunch of dill
1 lemon, finely sliced
freshly ground black pepper
rocket and lemon wedges, to serve

Serves 4

1. Preheat the oven to 230°C/gas mark 8. Put the salt in a mixing bowl and add the oregano and mint. Mix well. Pour in 150ml of cold water and mix into a paste.

2. Spread a large handful of salt onto a baking tray lined with baking paper and place the fish on top. Season the fish with black pepper and stuff with the garlic, dill and lemon. Cover with the rest of the salt and pack it tightly all over the fish so that it is sealed in a dome of salt. Cook in the oven for 20–25 minutes, or until a skewer inserted into the centre comes out hot. Leave for 10 minutes to rest.

3. To serve, crack the salt and pull it away from the fish. Remove the filling from the cavity and discard. Pull the skin away and carefully pick off the juicy flesh. Serve immediately with handfuls of rocket and lemon wedges.

Fisherman's Stew

Served in the little villages surrounding the beautiful seaside town of Marmaris on the western coast of Turkey, this sumptuous stew is made as a hearty meal for the local fishermen after a long day at sea. A base of tomatoes, onions and lemon is cooked with a few spices and the catch of the day. I use a mixture of seafood – whole red mullet, huge prawns and soft cod cheeks, which you can replace with any white fish you like. The stew cooks quickly, so this is great for a midweek dinner party.

2 tablespoons olive oil
1 onion, finely chopped
2 celery sticks, chopped
2 garlic cloves, finely sliced
2 bay leaves
½ teaspoon Turkish pepper flakes
½ teaspoon freshly ground black pepper
2 tablespoons red pepper paste
250ml boiling water
a pinch of saffron
½ teaspoon caster sugar
1 cinnamon stick (about 5cm)
400g tin chopped tomatoes
juice of ½ a lemon
2 red mullet (about 150g each), washed and cleaned
8 large king prawns, shells on
175g cod cheeks (or any white fish), cut into bite-sized pieces
a handful of finely chopped flat-leaf parsley leaves
sea salt

Serves 4

1. Heat the oil in a large frying pan over a medium heat and add the onion and celery. Cook, stirring occasionally, for 7–8 minutes until really golden and soft. Add the garlic, bay leaves, Turkish pepper and black pepper and mix well. Cook for 10 seconds until fragrant.

2. Meanwhile, mix the red pepper paste with the boiling water. Add the saffron, stir and then leave for a few minutes for the saffron to infuse. Pour into the pan with the onion and add the sugar, cinnamon, tomatoes, lemon juice and a good pinch of salt. Mix well. Cover, reduce the heat to low and cook for 20 minutes so that the flavours develop.

3. Place the red mullet into the stew. Cover and cook for 8–10 minutes until the fish is half cooked. Flip the fish over, cover and cook for another 8–10 minutes. Scatter over the prawns and cod cheeks, cover and cook for 8–10 minutes more until the prawns are coral pink and the cod cooked through. Sprinkle over the parsley and serve immediately.

Mussel *Pilav*

Throughout coastal towns in Turkey, you will find little carts selling *midye dolmasi*. This classic street food is made from huge mussels that are stuffed with *pilav* and served with a slice of lemon to squeeze over the top – rather like a food version of a tequila shot. Although they taste divine, stuffing mussels is a very time-consuming pursuit, so I created this dish as an alternative. The mussels are cooked and the liquor used as a stock for a simple *pilav*. The mussels are then returned to the finished rice and served with lemon wedges.

700g mussels, picked
and cleaned
350ml boiling water
2 tablespoons olive oil
1 onion, finely chopped
25g pine nuts
2 garlic cloves, finely chopped
40g raisins
300g basmati rice
2 teaspoons freshly ground
black pepper
½ teaspoon ground cinnamon
1½ teaspoons allspice
2 handfuls of finely chopped
flat-leaf parsley leaves
sea salt
lemon wedges, to serve

Serves 4

1. Put the mussels in a saucepan, add the boiling water and bring to the boil over a high heat. Cover and leave for 1–2 minutes, until the mussels have opened. Drain into a mixing bowl, reserving the liquor. Top up the stock with boiling water so that you have 700ml of liquid for the rice. Discard any mussels that have not opened.

2. Heat the oil in the same pan over a medium heat and add the onion and pine nuts. Cook, stirring occasionally, for 4–5 minutes until the nuts are golden and the onion translucent. Add the garlic and cook for 10 seconds until fragrant. Add the raisins and cook for 30 seconds more. Add the rice, black pepper, cinnamon and allspice. Pour in the hot stock and stir gently. Cover, reduce the heat to low and cook for 12–15 minutes until all the liquid has been absorbed. Season with salt and add the parsley. Mix with a fork.

3. Tip the mussels onto the rice in the pan and cover with a clean tea towel. Put the lid back on and leave for 10 minutes. This will help the rice fluff up and the mussels warm through. Serve immediately with masses of lemon wedges for squeezing over the top.

chapter

8

vegetarian

The vegetables used in Turkish cooking are fresh, seasonal and local.

Head to any local market and you will see piles of shiny purple aubergines, bright red peppers, juicy tomatoes, long, gnarled Turkish green peppers, sunshine-orange pumpkins, courgettes and much more. Turkey may be better known for its meaty kebabs and *köfte*, but the vegetables used in Turkish cooking are always fresh, seasonal and local, and prepared in a simple yet effective way, making the country's vegetable dishes something very special.

The most basic Turkish vegetable dish is a hearty stew made from onions, garlic, green peppers, tomatoes and whatever seasonal vegetables are available. This would be a simple dinner served hot, with rice and cold yogurt on the side. But this is just the start. There is so much more to discover; fluffy Herby Courgette Fritters (see page 194), barley stews perfumed with dried mint, or fresh peppers cooked in olive oil with a little tomato and a hell of a lot of garlic. In this chapter you will find a selection of beautiful dishes to bring the humble vegetable to your table in true Turkish style.

Kabak Mücver – Herby Courgette Fritters

Kabak mücver are served as a *meze* dish throughout Turkey. The seasonings change a little from region to region – extra chilli pepper in the east and more fresh herbs in the west – but they are always cooked in the summer when the courgettes are ripe and plentiful. To get them perfect every time, make sure that you wring all the excess moisture out of the courgettes before you put them in the batter. This will stop the fritters breaking apart when you cook them and give them a more intense flavour. In Turkey, they would use a crumbly cheese like *beyaz peynir* for this recipe. It has a salty flavour similar to feta cheese, which I find works just as well.

500g courgettes, finely grated
4 spring onions, finely chopped
2 handfuls of finely chopped flat-leaf parsley leaves
a handful of finely chopped dill
1 teaspoon dried mint
1 teaspoon Turkish pepper flakes
140g plain flour
2 eggs, separated
120g feta cheese
4 tablespoons olive oil
sea salt and freshly ground black pepper
lemon wedges, to serve

Serves 4

1. Put the grated courgettes in a sieve and squeeze them between your hands to get out all the moisture. Give them a really good going over so they look a bit battered. Put them into a mixing bowl and add the spring onions, parsley, dill, mint, Turkish pepper flakes and a good pinch of salt and black pepper. Sift over the flour and add the egg yolks. Crumble over the feta and mix well.

2. In a separate bowl, whisk the egg whites into soft peaks. Fold them into the batter so that they are completely incorporated.

3. Heat a little of the oil in a non-stick frying pan over a medium heat. Spoon in 2–3 tablespoons of the mixture. Shake the pan so that the mixture settles, then fry gently for 2–2 ½ minutes on each side, or until golden and cooked through. Top the pancakes with any leftover spring onions, feta and herbs, and serve immediately with lemon wedges.

Kale, Spinach, Pomegranate and Walnuts

Originally from Aleppo and recreated in eastern Turkey, this simple combination of greens, spices, softened onions and pomegranate is a classic. I have slightly modernised my version with a mixture of kale and spinach, and added fresh pomegranate seeds to add colour and a lovely sweet-sour hit. When you fry the onions, let them cook long and slow so that they turn into a sweet, sticky mess. It's this flavour and crispy texture that makes the finished dish so delicious.

200g kale
520g spinach
2 tablespoons butter
3 onions, finely sliced
25g walnuts, lightly crushed
a handful of chopped dill
½ teaspoon Turkish pepper flakes
¼ teaspoon ground cinnamon
2 tablespoons pomegranate molasses
2 tablespoons olive oil
juice of ½ lemon
¼ teaspoon caster sugar
100g pomegranate seeds
sea salt and freshly ground black pepper

Serves 4

1. Blanch the kale in a pan of boiling water for 3–4 minutes until soft. Blanch the spinach for 1–2 minutes. Drain both and refresh under cold running water. Drain thoroughly, wringing any excess moisture out with your hands.

2. Meanwhile, heat the butter in a pan over a medium heat and add the onions. Stir well and reduce the heat to low. Cook, shaking the pan occasionally, for 20–25 minutes until the onions are crispy. Remove from the pan and drain on kitchen paper.

3. Put the kale and spinach into a mixing bowl and add the walnuts, dill, Turkish pepper flakes and cinnamon.

4. Whisk the pomegranate molasses, oil, lemon juice, sugar and a good pinch of salt and black pepper together in a small mixing bowl. Pour over the kale and mix everything together. Tip the salad onto a serving dish. Top with the pomegranate seeds and fried onions and serve immediately.

Taze Fasulye – Green Beans with Tomatoes and Olive Oil

Cooked in homes and restaurants across Turkey, *taze fasulye* is a staple dish that is served as a side to a main meal or as part of a *meze*. The beans are cooked slowly in a mix of onions, garlic, tomatoes, red pepper paste and plenty of olive oil. They are then left to cool and served at room temperature, a typical way to prepare and serve many basic vegetable dishes in Turkey. This dish works well as a side to salads and grilled fish. Add a drizzle of good-quality extra virgin olive oil just before serving for a great finish.

4 tablespoons olive oil
2 onions, finely sliced
350g green beans, topped and tailed and cut in half
3 tablespoons red pepper paste
3 tomatoes, skinned and finely chopped
2 garlic cloves, finely chopped
½ teaspoon Turkish pepper flakes
1 teaspoon caster sugar
sea salt
extra virgin olive oil, to serve

Serves 4

1. Heat the oil in a pan over a medium heat and add the onions. Fry for 5–6 minutes until golden and soft.

2. Add the green beans, red pepper paste, tomatoes, garlic, Turkish pepper flakes and sugar, and mix everything together thoroughly. Cover, reduce the heat to low and cook for 35–40 minutes, or until the beans are soft. Remove from the heat and leave to cool to room temperature before serving drizzled with extra virgin olive oil.

Stewed Kale, Chickpeas and Bulgur

I first ate this hearty stew in Adana, in the Mediterranean region. It was made using purslane, a wonderful green that looks like lamb's leaf lettuce but has a firmer texture. Sadly, you can't get hold of it in the UK, so I adapted the recipe to be a bit more supermarket-friendly and opted for kale, which has a firm texture and irony taste. This stew is rich and healthy and very filling. I love it served piping hot with an extra squeeze of lemon. It also works really well served at room temperature. It mellows a little and the bulgur wheat's nutty taste develops still further.

4½ tablespoons olive oil
1 red onion, finely chopped
1 Turkish green pepper, finely sliced
2 garlic cloves, finely sliced
150g chickpeas, drained and rinsed
150g green lentils, drained and rinsed
1 tablespoon tomato purée
1 tablespoon red pepper paste
500ml hot vegetable stock (made from 1 stock cube)
50g bulgur wheat
200g kale
1 teaspoon dried mint
½ teaspoon Turkish pepper flakes
juice of ½ lemon
sea salt

Serves 4

1. Heat 2 tablespoons of the oil in a large pan over a medium heat and add the onion, green pepper and garlic. Fry for 4–5 minutes until translucent.

2. Add the chickpeas, lentils, tomato purée, red pepper paste, stock, bulgur, kale and a good pinch of salt. Mix together. Reduce the heat to low, cover and simmer for 18–20 minutes, or until the bulgur has swelled and the sauce thickened.

3. Meanwhile, heat the remaining oil in a small frying pan over a medium heat. Add the mint and Turkish pepper flakes. Remove from the heat, mix and leave to infuse for 30 seconds. Pour the flavoured oil into the cooked stew and add the lemon juice. Mix well and serve immediately.

Tarhana Soup

Made in villages high up in the mountains across Turkey, *tarhana çorbasi* is a silky and creamy winter soup. Summer vegetables, including peppers, tomatoes and garlic, are blended together with thick yogurt. This is then wrapped in muslin and hung to dry out over several weeks. The dry ball is then broken up into a powder that is stored for use during the harsh winter months. The flavourful mix is rehydrated and served hot with lots of lemon juice, butter and mint. I decided to simplify the process and developed a creamy roasted vegetable soup inspired by traditional *tarhana*, with yogurt, butter and dried mint. The essence is there and I can't get enough of it.

3 red peppers, deseeded and quartered
4 red onions, halved and each half cut into quarters
6 garlic cloves
6 tomatoes, halved
5 tablespoons olive oil
3 teaspoons dried mint
2 teaspoons dried oregano
1 teaspoon Turkish pepper flakes
100g Greek yogurt
250ml boiling water
25g butter
sea salt and freshly ground black pepper

Serves 4

1. Preheat the oven to 180°C/gas mark 4. Put the red peppers, onions, garlic and tomatoes in a roasting tray. Pour over 4 tablespoons of the oil and add 1 teaspoon of the dried mint, the oregano and ½ teaspoon of the Turkish pepper flakes. Season with salt and black pepper and mix together thoroughly.

2. Arrange the vegetables so that the tomatoes are sitting at the top, cut side-up, and drizzle over the remaining oil. Roast for 35–40 minutes until soft and a little golden. Leave to cool.

3. Tip the roasted vegetables into a food processor or blender and make sure to scrape out all the lovely oil and juices. Blend for 4–5 minutes until completely smooth. Pour into a saucepan and stir in the yogurt and a good pinch of salt. Add the boiling water and mix together. Cover and heat over a low heat for 15–20 minutes, stirring occasionally, until lovely and hot.

4. Heat the butter in a small saucepan over a medium heat until bubbling. Add the remaining dried mint and Turkish pepper flakes. Ladle the soup into warmed bowls and drizzle the infused butter over the top. Serve immediately.

Yogurt Soup

In Turkey, during the festival of *Kurban Bayramı* or *Eid Mubarek*, a lamb is slaughtered and given away to friends, family and the poor. The meat you receive is then used to make a family meal. Like many Turkish meals it begins with a soup, and along the Black Sea this simple yogurt soup is served as a starter. The creamy blandness is what makes it so special. Yogurt is enriched with egg yolk and then mixed with hot water and rice. It has to be stirred, like a risotto, for 20–25 minutes so that the rice cooks really slowly and over-swells, making the soup really thick and comforting.

400g Greek yogurt
1 egg yolk
1 tablespoon plain flour
150g basmati rice, washed
1 litre boiling water
1 tablespoon dried mint
1 tablespoon olive oil
sea salt
lemon wedges, to serve

Serves 4–6

1. Scoop the yogurt into a large saucepan. Add the egg yolk, flour and 120ml of cold water and whisk together. Pour in another 280ml of cold water and whisk again.

2. Add the rice and the boiling water. Cook over a medium heat, stirring continuously, for 20–25 minutes until thick. You will know when the soup is ready because the second you stop stirring it will start bubbling.

3. Add the mint, olive oil and a generous pinch of salt. Mix well. Reduce the heat to low and cook, stirring occasionally, for 5 minutes so that the flavours infuse. Serve immediately with lemon wedges.

Sebze Güveç – Vegetable Stew

Sebze güveç is served in different guises across Turkey, using fresh vegetables during the summer or intense dried aubergines, courgettes and peppers in the winter. Flavours change across the country: they are lighter in the west and spicier and rich in the east. This version uses the wonderful flavours of western Turkey – saffron, olives, and garlic. The new potatoes in the stew cook slowly and soak up all the flavours, while masses of chopped parsley freshens it all up at the end.

2 tablespoons olive oil
1 onion, finely sliced
500g new potatoes, halved and quartered
2 courgettes, halved and roughly chopped
1 red pepper, deseeded and roughly chopped
3 garlic cloves, finely chopped
400g tin chopped tomatoes
400g tin chickpeas, drained and rinsed
80g pitted black olives
2 tablespoons red pepper paste
2 teaspoons Turkish pepper flakes
1 teaspoon ground cumin
1½ teaspoon dried oregano
a pinch of saffron
300ml boiling water
a large handful of finely chopped flat-leaf parsley
sea salt and freshly ground black pepper

Serves 4

1. Heat the oil in a large saucepan over a medium heat. Add the onion and cook, stirring occasionally, for 3–4 minutes until soft.

2. Add the potatoes, courgettes, red pepper, garlic, tomatoes, chickpeas, olives, red pepper paste, Turkish pepper flakes, cumin, oregano, saffron and a good pinch of salt and black pepper. Pour in the boiling water and mix everything together thoroughly. Cover, reduce the heat to low and cook for 45 minutes.

3. Remove the lid, mix well and cook for 15 minutes so that the sauce thickens. Stir in the parsley, mix together and serve immediately.

Blackened Cauliflower

Although not classically Turkish, this blackened cauliflower has all the big flavours of eastern Turkey. The cauliflower softens in the oven and takes on a smoky flavour, while the garlicky yogurt and spicy butter add different tastes, textures and temperatures. I love the mix of hot and cold in this recipe; it's what makes it so unique. Serve it as a starter or *meze* dish, or, my favourite, with flatbread and plenty of finely sliced onions and chopped parsley.

1 cauliflower, cut into florets
2 tablespoons vegetable oil
½ teaspoon Turkish pepper flakes
150g Greek yogurt
juice of ½ lemon
1 tablespoon butter
1 teaspoon tomato purée
sea salt and freshly ground black pepper

Serves 4

1. Preheat the oven to 200°C/gas mark 6. Put the cauliflower florets into a mixing bowl and add the oil, half the Turkish pepper flakes and a good pinch of salt and black pepper. Mix well and tip onto a baking dish. Roast for 40–45 minutes until charred and tender. Set to one side to cool.

2. Meanwhile, put the yogurt into a mixing bowl and add the lemon juice and a good pinch of salt. Mix well.

3. Put the butter, tomato purée, the remaining Turkish pepper flakes and a pinch of salt into a small saucepan. Mix together and heat over a low heat until melted.

4. To serve, spread the yogurt onto a serving dish. Place the cauliflower over the top and drizzle over the hot butter. Serve immediately.

Garlicky Okra

This simple dish is a classic side to delicious dinners all over Turkey. I love how simple it is and how beautifully the flavours marry: rich, garlicky okra, smothered in a sticky sauce that has a very light lemony fragrance. Traditionally, this would be served at room temperature, but I prefer it hot from the pan. Sometimes I add a handful of chopped mint to freshen it up. I find this works particularly well during the hot summer barbecue months.

2 tablespoons olive oil
1 onion, finely sliced
3 garlic cloves, finely sliced
4 tomatoes, skinned and finely chopped
½ teaspoon caster sugar
350g okra, halved
75ml boiling water
juice of ½ a lemon
sea salt and freshly ground black pepper

Serves 4

1. Heat the oil in a frying pan over a medium heat. Add the onion and cook, stirring occasionally, for 5–6 minutes until golden. Add the garlic and fry for 30 seconds until fragrant.

2. Tip in the tomatoes. Season with salt and black pepper, add the sugar and mix well. Cook, stirring occasionally, for 3–4 minutes so that the tomatoes start to break down.

3. Add the okra and pour in the boiling water. Add the lemon juice and mix well. Cover, reduce the heat to low and simmer, stirring occasionally, for 10–12 minutes, or until the okra is tender and the sauce really thick. Serve immediately.

Aegean Aubergine *Pilav*

Sitting outside an old stone house on a warm summer's evening in the sleepy village of Alaçati, with honeysuckle and bougainvillea spilling down from the roof, we tucked into an incredible meal cooked by Gökçen Adar, one of Turkey's finest chefs. He made a selection of beautiful *meze* dishes, a delicate lamb stew with white beans and a fabulous aubergine *pilav*: classic Aegean food. This *pilav* is really light and peppery, and perfect as a side dish for a big meal, but it is also great as a simple weeknight supper.

4 tablespoons olive oil
1 aubergine, cut into 7.5cm pieces
4 spring onions, finely sliced
4 tomatoes, peeled and finely chopped
300g long-grain rice
55g pitted black olives
2 teaspoons freshly ground black pepper
700ml boiling water
a handful of finely chopped flat-leaf parsley leaves
30g pine nuts
sea salt

Serves 4

1. Pour the oil into a saucepan and add the aubergines. Mix well and heat over a medium heat. Cook, stirring regularly, for 8–10 minutes, or until the aubergines start turning golden.

2. Add the spring onions, mix well and cook for another 1–2 minutes to soften. Add the tomatoes, mix well and cook for 4–5 minutes, stirring occasionally, until they start to break down.

3. Tip the rice into the pan and add the olives and black pepper. Mix everything together carefully. Pour in the boiling water and give a quick stir. Cover, reduce the heat to low and cook for 10–12 minutes, or until the rice has absorbed all the water.

4. Remove the pan from the heat and cover with a clean tea towel. Put the lid back on and leave to stand for 10 minutes. This will help the rice fluff up.

5. Season the *pilav* with salt and add half the parsley and pine nuts. Gently mix together using a fork. Tip the *pilav* onto a serving dish, top with the remaining parsley and pine nuts, and serve immediately.

Pepper *Dolma*

Dolma is loved across Turkey. Peppers, courgettes, aubergines and cabbage can all be *dolma*'d. The process involves stuffing the vegetables with a rice, nut and herb mix, then cooking them slowly until the rice is tender and the vegetables soft. For this pepper *dolma* I have used a classic, slightly sweet Ottoman recipe for the filling, and stuffed it into British-style red peppers. In Turkey, they would use small green peppers that have a sweet flavour, not like the bitter green version we get here. Fill the peppers halfway to leave plenty of room for the rice to expand.

3 tablespoons olive oil
3 onions, finely chopped
1 tablespoon tomato purée
1 tablespoon red pepper paste
20g pine nuts
35g raisins
1 teaspoon caster sugar
1½ teaspoons ground cinnamon
a small handful of finely chopped mint leaves
a small handful of finely chopped flat-leaf parsley leaves
a small handful of finely chopped dill
120g basmati rice
4 red peppers
500ml boiling water
sea salt

Serves 4

1. Heat the oil in a large frying pan over a medium heat and add the onions. Cook, stirring occasionally, for 8–10 minutes until really golden. Add the tomato purée, red pepper paste, pine nuts, raisins, sugar, cinnamon and a good pinch of salt. Mix together thoroughly. Add the herbs and rice and mix together. Reduce the heat to low and cook for 2–3 minutes so that the rice can absorb any moisture.

2. Meanwhile, slice three-quarters of the way around the top of the peppers. Carefully pull open the tops and remove the seeds. Stuff a few spoons of the rice into each pepper and sit them upright in a saucepan. Pour the boiling water into the pan, cover and cook over a low heat for 1–1 ½ hours, or until the rice is tender. You should be able push a skewer through the side of the pepper and into the centre really easily. Serve immediately.

Cevizli Erişte – Walnut Pasta

During the cold winter months in Anatolia, homemade noodles that look like short tagliatelle are served with walnuts, butter and cheese. In this region of Turkey, agriculture is based on wheat, and fresh noodles are made in the summer and stored for the winter. This simple dish is hearty and warming, and perfect to keep energy levels up. So popular is *cevizli erişte* that it is cooked across Turkey for a quick midweek family meal. A light, stringy cheese is stirred into the pasta – the type used changes regionally, but for this recipe I have used mozzarella, as it is easy to find and has the perfect texture and mild flavour for this recipe.

400g tagliatelle
75g butter
200g grated mozzarella
75g walnuts, lightly crushed
1 teaspoon freshly ground black pepper
1 teaspoon Turkish pepper flakes
½ teaspoon dried mint
sea salt

Serves 4

1. Cook the pasta in a large pan of salted boiling water according to packet instructions. Drain and return to the pan.

2. Add the butter, cheese, walnuts, black pepper, Turkish pepper flakes, mint and a good pinch of salt. Mix everything together thoroughly and serve immediately.

Freekeh *Pilav*

Freekeh is an ancient grain that has been used in kitchens across the Middle East for centuries. It is actually wheat that is picked young and sun dried. The stalks are then set on fire so that the grains smoke. The resulting freekeh has a firm texture and a smoky, nutty flavour. It works fantastically in soups, stews and salads, and in place of rice in a *pilav* it is both comforting and wholesome. Freekeh *pilav* is often served in Turkey with grilled *köfte* and vegetables. I particularly love it with my Aubergine *köfte* (see page 79) and a crisp green salad.

2 tablespoons olive oil
1 onion, finely chopped
2 garlic cloves, finely chopped
2 tablespoons red pepper paste
2 tablespoons tomato purée
700ml hot vegetable stock
200g freekeh, washed
and drained
1 teaspoon freshly ground
black pepper
a handful of finely chopped
flat-leaf parsley leaves
50g pine nuts, toasted
sea salt

Serves 4

1. Heat the oil in a non-stick saucepan over a medium heat. Add the onion and cook, stirring occasionally, for 4–5 minutes until a little golden. Add the garlic and cook for 10 seconds until fragrant.

2. Meanwhile, whisk the red pepper paste and tomato purée into the stock.

3. Tip the freekeh into the onions and mix well. Pour over the stock and add the black pepper. Mix well, cover, reduce the heat to low and cook gently for 35–40 minutes. If it looks a little too wet, cook for a few minutes with the lid off.

4. Season with salt and stir in the parsley. Scatter over the pine nuts and serve immediately.

9
desserts

Turkish people have a real sweet tooth.

They love eating something sweet after every meal, even breakfast, and, in Istanbul, one of the most popular things to do after a night out is to have a late-night dessert on the way home. Many Turks will say a meal is not complete until you have eaten something sweet. There are so many incredible *tatli* (desserts) in Turkish cuisine, in addition to the little sweet treats and pastries that are enjoyed with tea and coffee throughout the day.

Baklava, a sticky, sweet, crispy pastry that is stuffed with nuts, is served in shops all over the country. Some of the best *baklava* comes from Gazientep in eastern Turkey, and I have had the pleasure of meeting one of the owners of Güllüoğlu, the biggest *baklava* chain in the country. Not only did he show me around his massive factory, he also told me about his new helicopter – apparently *baklava* is worth its weight in gold (or helicopters).

Another popular treat is an old Ottoman dessert called *muhallebi*, a custard that is flavoured in many different ways or served as a creamy rice pudding. Chocolate is also adored and is eaten as a chocolate *supangle*, which is like a mousse, as well as in lots of chocolate cakes and pastries. At home, simple desserts like rice pudding and a chocolate biscuit dessert (like Tülay's Chocolate Pudding, see page 221) are more likely to be served. The Turkish also love *helva*, a stunning Middle Eastern sweet that is made in two ways; hard *helva* is tahini based, while soft *helva* is made with flour and sugar and is served at funerals.

In this chapter I have handpicked some of my favourite Turkish desserts that are simple to make at home. They include a wonderfully easy Honey *Baklava* (see page 218) that only takes a few minutes to prepare and Mosaic Cake (see page 233), which is just about the best chocolate dessert in the world.

Honey *Baklava*

Like many of the oldest dishes in Turkey, the origins of *baklava* are slightly blurred. Records from the Turks, Ottomans, Byzantines, Greeks and Romans all make claims to this sticky sweet treat. In Turkey today, *baklava* is made in shops using thin layers of pastry that are stuffed with nuts. The tins of *baklava* are doused in melted butter and cooked in wood-fired ovens until crispy. Finally, boiling hot sugar syrup is poured over the top and the tins are left to cool. In Gaziantep they grow the best pistachios in Turkey, and different varieties of bright green *baklava* are made. Along the Black Sea, hazelnut *baklava* is sold instead. *Baklava* is served with coffee or tea for a mid-afternoon snack, and if you are ever invited to dinner with a Turkish family, take freshly made *baklava* and you will be an instant hit. The traditional recipe is too time-consuming to recreate at home, so I was inspired to make a version more suitable for the home kitchen, using shop-bought filo pastry that is rolled up and baked. The end result looks great and the flavour is just as good.

125g extra-thick double cream

75g unsalted butter, plus extra for brushing

1 tablespoon vegetable oil

55g walnuts, lightly crushed

55g blanched almonds, lightly crushed

40g soft light brown sugar

6 sheets of filo pastry

5 tablespoons runny honey

1 teaspoon ground cinnamon

Serves 6–8

1. Preheat the oven to 180°C/gas mark 4. Put the cream, butter and oil in a small saucepan and heat over a low heat, stirring occasionally, for 5–6 minutes or until completely melted. Remove from the heat and set aside.

2. Mix the walnuts, almonds and sugar in a mixing bowl.

3. Take a sheet of pastry and brush it with the melted butter mixture. Fold the bottom edge up so that it reaches about three-quarters of the way up towards the centre. Scatter a line of nuts and sugar about 2.5cm in from the bottom. Fold in the sides and roll up from the bottom into a cigar shape. Slice on an angle and place the cut slices in rows in a buttered ovenproof dish. Repeat with the remaining pastry and filling. Brush the top with melted butter and bake for 30–35 minutes, or until golden and crispy.

4. Drizzle with the honey and sprinkle over the cinnamon. Leave to absorb for at least 30 minutes before serving.

Tülay's Chocolate Pudding

Like all the best cuisines, Turkish cooking has evolved and modern recipes have been developed. This simple chocolate pudding is the perfect example. It is modern home cooking that has been adopted across Turkey, and something I will insist is in the fridge when I visit family on the Black Sea. Shop-bought cookies are blended to a fine rubble and mixed with cream. Like a cheesecake, this base is 'set' in the fridge and then covered in a thick chocolate sauce. It is heavenly and a perfect treat for the Turkish sweet tooth.

350g chocolate chip cookies
55g walnut pieces, plus a few extra for topping
675ml double cream
4 tablespoons icing sugar
100g dark chocolate (70% cocoa solids), chopped
50g unsalted butter
2 tablespoons runny honey

Serves 6

1. Tip the cookies into a food processor and blend until fine. Pour into a mixing bowl and add the walnuts.

2. Pour 500ml of the cream into a separate mixing bowl and add the icing sugar. Whip into soft peaks using an electric whisk, then fold into the biscuit mix. Tip everything into a shallow dish. Spoon it in gently so it stays light. Cover with clingfilm and refrigerate for 2 hours.

3. Meanwhile, put the chocolate, remaining cream, butter and honey in a small sauce pan over over a medium heat. Stir occasionally, until the chocolate melts and it forms a velvety sauce.

4. To serve, put a generous portion of the cookie mixture into a bowl and pour over the warm chocolate sauce. Serve immediately.

Hazelnut Biscuits

Some of the best hazelnuts in the world come from the Black Sea region of Turkey, where they grow in abundance and are used to flavour a variety of different desserts, including sticky *baklava* and these crunchy biscuits. The base is made from a mixture of flour and ground almonds. This is topped with crushed hazelnuts that turn golden in the oven. As in Turkey, serve these delicious biscuits with hot *çay* for the perfect afternoon snack.

250g unsalted butter
350g golden caster sugar
2 eggs
1 teaspoon vanilla extract
300g plain flour
2 teaspoons bicarbonate of soda
50g ground almonds
2 tablespoons hazelnuts, finely ground
sea salt

Makes 20 biscuits

1. Preheat the oven to 180°C/gas mark 4 and line a baking tray with baking paper.

2. Put the butter and sugar into a food processor or blender and blend until smooth. Add the eggs and vanilla and blend until fluffy and light in colour. Add the flour, bicarbonate of soda, almonds and a pinch of salt. Mix together into a firm paste.

3. Put 2–3 tablespoons of the mixture onto the prepared baking tray. Leave plenty of space around the first biscuit for it to spread out in the oven and repeat with more of the mix. Top each one with a sprinkling of hazelnuts and bake for 10–12 minutes until slightly golden. Remove from the oven and set aside to cool before serving.

Revani – Semolina Lemon Cake

Revani is a victory cake that was named when the Ottomans conquered the Armenian city of Yerevan. It is a classic dessert that is now served all over Turkey and the Middle East. A baked semolina cake is soaked in a thick sugar syrup until it turns into a moist, soft, sticky sponge. To get the *revani* just right, make sure that you pour the hot sugar syrup over the top of the cooled cake in batches, so that all the syrup can be absorbed. I have seen *revani* served with whole almonds, ground pistachios and even grated coconut on top. This recipe is for the classic version without any kind of topping, as I think it needs nothing else.

160g semolina flour
160g plain flour
3 teaspoons baking powder
120g unsalted butter, plus extra for greasing
150g caster sugar
3 eggs, separated
1 teaspoon vanilla extract
1 teaspoon orange extract

For the sugar syrup
125g caster sugar
juice of 1 orange
juice of 1 lemon

Serves 6–8

1. Preheat the oven to 180°C/gas mark 4 and butter a 15cm square baking dish or tin.

2. Put the semolina, flour and baking powder into a mixing bowl.

3. Put the butter and sugar into a food processor or blender and blend to a light consistency. Add the egg yolks, one at a time, and the vanilla and orange extracts. Continue to blitz until you have a really light mixture. Add the flour mixture and blend until smooth.

4. Whisk the egg whites into soft peaks and fold into the cake mixture. Pour into the prepared dish or tin and bake for 25–30 minutes until the cake is light brown on top and you can remove a skewer cleanly from the centre. Set aside to cool.

5. Meanwhile make the sugar syrup. Put the sugar in a pan with 125ml of cold water. Add the orange and lemon juices and bring to the boil over a medium heat. Once bubbling, reduce the heat to low and simmer gently for 5 minutes.

6. Poke lots of holes into the top of the baked cake using a skewer and pour over half the syrup. Leave for 10 minutes and then pour over the remaining syrup. Leave to cool for at least 30 minutes before serving.

Sac Arası – Filo Twirls with Walnuts and Cinnamon

This is my version of the *sac arasi* puddings – a swirled, thin pastry filled with walnuts and sugar and doused in a sweet syrup – that I tasted one very cold day in Konya. It was great, but a bit teeth tingling for me, so I decided to make my own with less sugar and a slightly more substantial filling. When you wrap up the *sac arasi*, it is best to be as random as you can with the filling – no neat lines here. The gaps will help stop too much of the filling from bursting as it cooks.

35g unsalted butter, plus
1 tablespoon for brushing
65g walnuts
70g caster sugar
4 sheets of filo pastry
flour, for dusting
1 teaspoon ground cinnamon
zest of ½ orange

Serves 4 - 6

1. Preheat the oven to 180°C/gas mark 4 and line a baking tray with buttered baking paper.

2. Melt 1 tablespoon of the butter in a small saucepan and set aside for brushing. Put the walnuts, 40g of the sugar and the rest of the butter into a food processor or blender and blend to a rough paste.

3. Take two filo pastry sheets and lay them on top of each other on a floured board. Spread half the filling in a broken line about 2cm in from the bottom. Roll the bottom of the pastry up over the filling and roll everything over once. Push all the remaining pastry down so it concertinas towards the roll of filling. With the filling in the middle, shape it into a very loose twirl or coil. Carefully transfer onto the prepared baking tray. Repeat with the rest of the pastry and filling. Brush the tops of the twirls with a little melted butter. Bake for 20 minutes until golden and crispy.

4. Meanwhile, heat the remaining sugar with 30ml water in a small saucepan over a medium heat. Once the sugar has dissolved, reduce the heat to low and bubble for 10 minutes, or until there is only about 2 tablespoons of liquid left. Spoon the sugar syrup over the cooked pastries. Sprinkle a pinch of cinnamon and a little orange zest over each twirl. Leave to cool for at least 30 minutes before serving.

Pomegranate and Walnut Rice Pudding

This is Turkish comfort food, tarted up thanks to a wonderful lady I bumped into one day in the stunning stone village of Alaçati. It was a religious holiday and she was taking dessert to her neighbours. Instead of putting the rice pudding under the grill to give it an almost crème brûlée finish as others do, she had put a vibrant array of fruit and nuts over the top. She very kindly offered me some of the pudding, and since then I have always made mine the same way.

120g basmati rice
3 tablespoons cornflour
750ml full-fat milk
250ml double cream
1 teaspoon vanilla extract
180g caster sugar
100g pomegranate seeds
60g dried apricots,
finely chopped
30g walnuts, lightly crushed
2 teaspoons ground cinnamon

Serves 4

1. Put the rice into a pan with 350ml of cold water and bring to the boil over a medium heat. Cover, reduce the heat to low and cook for 15 minutes until all the water has been absorbed.

2. Whisk the cornflour with a few tablespoons of the milk. Pour the rest of the milk and the cream into the cooked rice. Add the cornflour paste, the vanilla and sugar. Mix well and cook, stirring occasionally, for 20 minutes until thick and creamy.

3. To serve, spoon the rice pudding into serving bowls or glasses and top each one with pomegranate seeds, apricots, walnuts and a good pinch of cinnamon. Serve immediately.

Mosaic Cake

Turkish people love eating chocolate and you can find a huge variety of chocolate desserts served in restaurants, pâtisseries and homes across the country. This simple chocolate torte, known as mosaic cake, is a homemade classic: biscuits are crushed up and folded into melted chocolate, giving the finished dish a tiled or mosaic-like appearance. Walnuts, hazelnuts and dry cherries lend more texture and a wonderful variety of flavours that work so well with dark chocolate. The mosaic cake sets really hard in the fridge, so make sure you take it out at least 30 minutes before serving to come to room temperature.

150g unsalted butter, plus extra for greasing
300g dark chocolate (70% cocoa solids), chopped
4 tablespoons runny honey
300g Rich Tea biscuits
50g walnuts, finely crushed
50g hazelnuts, finely crushed
100g dried cherries, roughly chopped
cocoa powder, to dust

Serves 8–10

1. Put the butter, chocolate and honey into a saucepan and heat over a low heat, stirring occasionally, until everything has melted together.

2. Tip the biscuits into a food processor or blender and blend until fine. Transfer to a mixing bowl. Add the walnuts, hazelnuts and dried cherries. Pour over the velvety smooth melted chocolate and fold everything together into a coarse mixture.

3. Spoon the mixture into a buttered 450g loaf tin and push everything down with the back of a spoon. Cover and refrigerate for 2 hours.

4. Remove from the fridge and leave for at least 30 minutes before serving. To serve, run a knife around the edge of the loaf tin to dislodge the cake. Place onto a wooden board and tip the torte out. Dust with cocoa powder and serve in thin slices.

Katmer Pastry

This sweet pastry is a typical breakfast dish served in Gaziantep, in the south east of Turkey, and is traditionally given as a gift the morning after a wedding from the groom's family to the bride's as a thank you for the festivities. The dough is made with flour, water and lots of oil and is very technical to prepare. It is kneaded and spun around, a little like a pizza, until wafer thin. I have used filo pastry to make it quicker to prepare at home. Traditional *katmer* is very sweet, but this version goes easy on the sugar and uses a little drizzle of honey at the end instead to give extra sweetness and help the final shower of pistachios stick to the sweet pastry.

4 squares of filo pastry
20g unsalted butter, melted
100g ground pistachios
8 teaspoons caster sugar
4 tablespoons thick clotted cream
runny honey, to serve

Makes 4 individual pastries

1. Preheat the oven to 200°C/gas mark 6 and line a baking tray with baking paper.

2. Take a square of filo pasty and lay it on a chopping board. Brush it lightly with butter. Sprinkle about 25g of the pistachios in a square in the centre of the filo pastry, leaving a 2cm gap around the edges. Scatter over 2 teaspoons of the sugar and dollop 1 tablespoon of the clotted cream over the nuts.

3. Fold the corners of the filo pastry into the centre to make a smaller square. Brush the top with a little more butter, then place onto the baking tray. Repeat with the remaining three pieces of pastry.

4. Bake for 10-12 minutes, or until lovely and golden. Remove from the oven and drizzle a little honey over each *katmer*. Scatter over the remaining pistachios and serve immediately.

index

index

Turkish delights

index

acknowledgements

Thanks to everyone in Turkey who has helped make this book happen: Saliha and Ishan, Tülay and all of the Aktas family, Göckçen Adar, Osman and Sebahat at ncirliev and everyone at Cafe LaLa. Thanks also to Hulya at Redmint Communications, Go Turkey and Pegasus Airlines for being so supportive.

Thanks to all of my family – Gregory-Smiths, Orringes and, of course, my M, Murat.

Also huge thanks to everyone at Kyle Books: Kyle and Judith for thinking this would work and Tara for holding my hand every step of the way.

Martin Poole, Rosie Reynolds, Wei Tang and Ruth Tyson, thank you for bringing my book to life and making it look so utterly beautiful.

And to my agent, Elly James, the ultimate voice of reason: hats off – you are wicked!